MEANS OF ESCAPE

by

Dolly M. Palmer

Penman Publishing, Inc.

First Published 2002
Penman Publishing, Inc.
4159 Ringgold Road, Suite 104
Chattanooga, Tennessee 37412

MEANS OF ESCAPE

by Dolly M. Palmer

ISBN: 0-9712808-6-X

Manufactured in the United States of America.

Printed by Penman Publishing, Inc.

Acknowledgements

To my God—for hearing my prayers and cries in the night. I survived because of You.

I would also like to thank the following very important people in my life:

To my parents—for understanding the importance of my telling this story, and for supporting me through it all.

To Eddie—I am blessed to have you as my brother, and I am honored to call you my friend.

To Ray and Mary Lee Hammond, my publishers—I could not have done this without you.

And finally:

To my love—Shawn.

In the words of Jim Brickman:

"All I want is to hold you forever.
All I need is you more every day.
You saved my heart from being broken apart.
You gave your love away,
and I'm thankful everyday
... for the gift."

I am blessed to have you in my life. You taught me the meaning of unconditional love. Thank you.

Dedication

This book is dedicated to all the women who were not as fortunate as I was.

Images of You

You ask me to write a poem about you,
capture your essence in black and white.
Do you want me to mention how handsome you are?
How your eyes are so very blue,
your grin so broad.
Shall I mention your high academic standing,
your future in engineering?
Can I talk about how beautiful you make me feel;
how secure I am when I'm with you,
or shall I tell the truth?

If I wrote the truth, I would have to mention
the scar on my heart
that matches the one on my face.
The way you laughed and ridiculed
as I lay helpless on the kitchen floor
crying
while you applauded and called me an actress.

To write a poem about you
I would have to remember you,
rewind my life to those moments
when I thought my life was truly over.

So there is no need to write about you,
you will haunt me forever.

Introduction

Once in your life you will read, see, or hear something that truly affects you. Maybe it's something that happened to you or someone you know. Maybe you can relate to it. Suddenly, you feel compelled to tell others about it. *You* become the heroine, the survivor, and feel an enormous amount of pride in yourself. You want to share *your* story now. For you have overcome the shame, the stereotypes, and are reborn into a new world: a world of understanding and of hope.

This is the story of a survivor: a survivor of emotional, physical and sexual abuse. This is the story of a woman who overcame the fears, and the threats . . . and lived.

This is my story.

PROLOGUE

When it was over, I wanted to forget. I wanted to go to a different place, become a different person. I couldn't look people in the eye because I thought they would see me as 'dirty.' After all, I had been abused; physically and sexually.

I spent my nights in the dark, hiding from the world. Was I also hiding from myself? I tried to keep busy with work, college, the bathroom tile, the kitchen curtains—anything to help me ignore the reality of my life. From now on I would be classified as a battered woman.

In college, I read countless books about abuse: domestic and substance. I saw the statistics and watched the videotapes from prominent psychologists and psychiatrists who talked about the battered woman and generalities of such. I listened to my professors' description of the typical abuser: an alcoholic, possibly with a drug addiction, who had a high school education, or none at all. He was a blue-collar worker, was not religious or family oriented. Maybe he had a bad childhood, or was abused himself. What about the battered woman? She was poor, uneducated, had children and spoke with a Southern drawl. With nowhere to go, she needed to stay in the relationship for the kids' sake, or for monetary reasons.

I found out the hard way that domestic violence is not class specific, nor is it race related or associated with lower educated individuals. I was not the stereotype.

Life unraveled before my eyes, and I watched an upper middle class, college-educated woman become a shell of her former self and spiral downward into a world of despair and destruction. I watched a middle class college-educated man destroy a woman's dreams. I watched him burn her diary; rape her body . . . and soul. He never drank, and never tried pot or cocaine. As a matter of fact, he'd never even tried a drug in his life. He was an intelligent man who held a relatively high position in his office, and maintained a high academic standing in college. He had what appeared to be a solid family unit—a rather well off family, one might say. So how can we generalize and stereotype when it comes to abuse?

Should we blame the woman for not getting out of the situation? Do we just shake our heads and walk away from the unfortunate and countless deaths of these women who *did* try to escape? Or do we turn the television off, close the newspaper, and forget . . . We, the abused, cannot forget.

And so it begins: the arduous task of healing oneself. As hard as I tried to go on with my life, I was taking one step forward and six steps backward. I was convinced that I had dealt with the pain, examined the reasons why I was involved in such an abnormal and cancerous relationship. Was it my lack of self-esteem, or his overabundance of charm that first attracted me to him? At nineteen years old, many women are still unsure of who they are. We read magazines that tell us how to be the sexiest, smartest, thinnest—we often look to others, subconsciously, to define who we are. We look up to those who exude confidence, independence and intelligence. In high school, we date the cutest boy, or the most popular, because that's the norm. We want acceptance. Does it matter that the cutest boy was sometimes mean to me? Does it matter that the most popular boy often asked where I was, if he called and I wasn't home? And after years of conditioning, do we become desensitized to this dating ritual?

As for me, I sometimes reflect back and ask if it was my belief over time that I deserved no better? I was so young—and yes, impressionable. But more importantly, after countless attacks and rapes, I was marred. He made me believe that nobody would ever want somebody like me. I believed him.

When I got the strength to walk away, I didn't realize that this was going to be a long road of recovery. I had convinced myself that once I was stronger, more independent, I would be able to forget the past and begin a bright future without the memory of him lingering. However, I soon found out that unless I actively dealt with the trauma, I could not further my own personal growth, nor would I ever maintain a healthy relationship with anyone.

It was hard to remember the pain. I didn't want to remember. It was in my past and I wanted to go on with my life. But the more I tried to go on, the more I would wake up in the middle of the night crying or thinking that my face was bruised, or that he had just raped me. The thought of talking about my situation with anyone, especially my family, was unbearable. I didn't want them to know the gory details of what actually had transpired during those years. Yes, they knew something was wrong. They tried time after time to warn me, to stop me from furthering the destructive pattern he had created. They worried, they cried. But unless I was ready to leave, there was nothing anyone could do. Nevertheless, they never knew about the rapes. They never had to see the black eyes and bloody lips. I covered them well.

When the relationship ended, I needed desperately to feel—I don't know, appreciated. I needed someone to validate my existence. I wanted somebody to tell me I was pretty or smart, or both. And yet I remained alone, for fear of humiliation and rejection.

Maybe I was afraid that I wasn't good enough for anybody else. After all, I was second-hand goods. Or so I thought. I wanted the attention that I wasn't even ready to give myself. I thought I could forget the past by letting somebody new into my future. It never worked. I found that in the first few weeks of a relationship, things were okay—not great by any stretch of the imagination, but just *okay.* I didn't talk about my past and didn't want to know about their past. When it got beyond dinner and a movie, I became scared. Intimacy frightened me. After all, I was never made love *to,* I was raped—repeatedly, and over a three-year period. I never knew the touch of a gentle hand or a warm and tender embrace. I never knew love. And above all, I thought I had been *tainted* in some twisted manner, where no man would want me, if they knew what he had done. I guess I just didn't want to see the expression on their faces when I told them. So I didn't—I just merely explained that I was the one with the problem; I wasn't ready for a serious relationship.

I made excuses for every one of the men I dated. *He was too possessive. He was too jealous. That guy just isn't right for me.* I kept putting off the fact that *I* was the one who had been abused, wanting to deny that I was still hurting inside. I had come so far, I thought. I graduated college with a double major and started a business career in the mutual fund industry. I was more confident with my appearance and inner self. But even I must admit, when looking back now, I knew there was an underlying problem—a fear if you will, that I didn't think I deserved to be loved. I made constant excuses for the men I dated.

Yes, in part it was because they really weren't the one for me, but mostly because I was afraid to let them in. I was afraid to let them know the real me—the *me* that can't sleep in darkness and carries a night light when she stays at a friend's house; the one who wakes from nightmares of abuse at *his* hands; the one who wonders if she will ever find a man understanding enough to get to know her strengths *and* weaknesses.

For those first two years, I struggled with the idea of therapy. I guess in the beginning, I was still in shock and just trying to get myself back slowly. I didn't want to relive the misery and thought that in time I would learn to forget. I later found that *forgetting* is merely another name for denial.

I did try counseling once. I was ready to admit being abused and ready to talk about it and move on with my life. I was tired of just going through the motions. And so I did. One night in January, I saw a woman therapist. I remember it being January, because it was four degrees below zero outside and we had thirteen inches of snow on the ground from the previous night. My appointment was at seven-thirty P.M., and my car was stalling the entire way, which was only about fifteen minutes away from home.

When I got there, I apologized for being a few minutes late. I noticed the woman was nonchalant about our first meeting and I got the impression that she would rather be someplace else. I should have left right there and then, because I was told (and I can't remember by whom) that if you get a bad feeling from the therapist upon first meeting him or her, then your best bet would be to find another therapist. Well, I didn't. I told her my family history; how many brothers I had, if I had any sisters, did my mother and I get along . . . blah, blah, blah. That took almost the entire hour. The final ten minutes I had left, she asked me about him. What did he look like? What first attracted me to him? (Did she really need to know this? I wondered.)

She thanked me for my time and walked me to the front door, whereupon we made another appointment for the following week. I knew then that I should not go back, but I didn't really know where else to go. I needed help. She was licensed and worked close to my home.

The following week I went back to see her. Upon my return, she spent the first ten minutes looking for the notes she had written down at my first visit. Then she proceeded to ask me to describe one of the incidents of abuse. As I began, I watched her facial expression, that of indifference. She pressed for further examples, and when I started to talk about the most serious one—where later I explained (lied) to my mother that I was in a car accident—the woman promptly looked at her watch and said, "Okay then. Time's up. See you next week?" And with that, she stood up and waited for me to compose myself.

I had begun to cry when I started talking about this painful incident. And now as I rose from the hard wooden chair, I was numb. I felt like I had been raped, yet again. Here was this *professional* woman, with a degree in psychology; a woman who would supposedly help me and she made no apologies for getting off her chair and standing by the door. I was hurt and furious all at the same time. That was my last experience with therapy.

Through reviewing some of my college psychology books, I found that what I have is called Post Traumatic Stress Disorder and Battered Woman's Syndrome. With PTSD the therapist is supposed to start off slowly with the client, asking general questions about the person, their childhood, family and friends, etc. Only after a relationship emerges between the client and therapist can the therapist begin to ask more personal questions, and slowly uncover the nature of the trauma. The therapist is supposed to build trust within the confines of the patient-therapist relationship. This woman did nothing of the kind. I decided to forget about counseling and put the past behind me—again.

It is my hope that *"Means of Escape"* will help women *and* men, who are involved or know someone involved in a domestic violence situation. It is my wish to let those people know that you can be saved. You can survive. I did.

However, it is not an easy road. I am finding that out, as I go . . . still. It is a healing *process;* a process that takes time and patience. When I finished this book, I thought I was done. I lived it and relived it again through my writing and thought I was completely healed. I came to find out that I wasn't. But that's okay, too. Being abused, at any level, is a traumatic and life-altering occurrence. Occasionally, I will wake from a bad nightmare. I will flinch when someone comes up behind me suddenly. It is a long road. But aren't you worth it?

1994

The red light was flashing on her answering machine as she entered the bedroom. She reached behind the teal satin curtains with lace trim and squinted as she lowered the beige shade on the window. The evening sun began to set before her and from the window she could see the leaves of autumn beginning to fall.

She lived in Scituate, a quaint town located in Massachusetts. It was so different from the bustling city of Boston where she worked. For over three years now, she had been working as an investment representative for one of the oldest mutual fund companies. How different it was from her earlier days in the work force. How different *she* was.

She was a college graduate, a member of the Alumni, and while in college had worked three part-time jobs totaling over forty-seven hours a week. Her jobs ranged from switchboard operator to counter girl in a dry-cleaning store, and she still maintained a grade point average of 3.4. Life was hard then. Her father told her the years of hard work would eventually pay off, and he was right.

She pulled on the closet door handle, catching her reflection in the mirrored door, and opened it. She reached for the light. *What would she wear,* she wondered? Tonight she was going to a dinner party with Shawn. They'd had to cancel the past three social events—the Stinson account. She had worked on it relentlessly for five months, giving up her social life and a portion of her time with her husband to win the trust of Mr. Stinson.

Nevertheless, she was late. Fingering through her clothes, she caught a glimpse of the gold watch on her left wrist that Shawn had given her on her last birthday. *I'll give him a quick call,* she thought, as she reached for the ivory phone on the oak night table. Shawn answered immediately, anticipating her call, and she began to ramble. "I'm sorry Honey, but I'm running a little behind schedule. I got caught up at the office . . . you know how it is." She was speaking, yet again, in that soft voice she often used in times like these. "I'll meet you there, okay? No, no, don't go out of your way. Stay in town and I'll be there in forty minutes."

Hanging up the receiver, her eye spotted the flashing light of the answering machine. *Didn't I already listen to this?* she thought hurriedly. Leaning toward the black machine and unbuttoning her blouse, she listened to the messages. *She would wear the black dress,* she decided, as she heard the woman's voice begin to speak.

"Grace Ryan, this is Mrs. Godfrey. I work for Nynex. There is a Mr. Robert Gagnon trying to reach you."

She was slipping on the black dress and suddenly stopped cold. Her legs started to tremble as she sat breathlessly on the queen size bed. She couldn't speak. She just closed her eyes and listened.

"Well your number is unlisted, Mrs. Ryan, so I couldn't give it to him. He asked if I could contact you and leave his number instead. His number is area code 305 . . . uh, let me see, 779-1342. Thank you, Mrs. Ryan. Good day."

As she sat motionless on the bed, her thoughts drifted to another time, another place, when her life had been so different from today...

PART I - THE BEGINNING

Chapter 1 - October 1987

Late again, I guess!" Grace laughed as she flew in through the glass entrance doors, leaving a trail of Soft Musk perfume blowing behind her. She was wearing a Chaus' double-breasted peach suit, tailored to fit her five-foot four-inch figure. Her dirty-blond hair was neatly pulled back in a French twist, held together with an ivory bow.

"Has my mom called down yet?" she asked as she signed the employees' sign-in sheet.

"Not yet. She probably hasn't realized yet that you're late," Robbie replied. Robbie was the Director of Security Operations in her mother's office building. It was an exposition center that housed such shows as the boat and home shows. People from all over the world came to see them. Robbie saw Grace every Tuesday, Thursday and on weekends when she worked the switchboard in her mother's office upstairs. He watched her speed down the parking lot on those afternoons and reach hurriedly for the sign-in sheet, as she explained each time why she was late. It became amusing to him and he looked forward to seeing her.

Robbie had worked for security for almost three years. It was a monotonous job, one without any real excitement. Except for the occasional fire-alarm sounding, his job was pretty boring. Grace brought life into his world.

She worked for her mother part-time. At nineteen, Grace had a full-time job as an executive assistant in an accounting firm and truly loved it. She was in charge of all quarterly financial statements, preparing the individual and corporate tax returns, and processing various other tax forms. It made her feel important to have such a position.

Grace graduated from high school tenth in her class. She studied writing, theater and the fundamental math and sciences. With the hope of climbing the work-force corporate ladder, she had turned down two scholarships from local colleges. Grace began to notice, however, that her colleagues were climbing faster than she was, despite the early mornings and late evenings spent at the office. She began to think that a college degree was necessary. Nevertheless, she was somewhat enthralled with her position and didn't want to give it up just yet to begin a four-year journey through college bliss.

"You know, Grace, if you went to college with me, you'd be making a lot more money when you graduate and you wouldn't need two jobs," Robbie yelled from across the exhibition hall, with a smile in his voice.

"Yeah, whatever," she smiled back, as she flew up the stairs to her mother's office. *What a cutie*, she thought, as she closed the door behind her. *Too bad he's taken.* Robbie was dating a girl from college. They had been dating for almost a year now. Although Grace never met her, she didn't like what she heard about her. It was something about the way Robbie acted when he talked about her. He was always quick-witted and charming, and yet when he talked about her, he became angry and fiercely emotional. Grace wondered what their story was.

After work that night, Grace locked the door behind her and walked quickly toward the front lobby. It was late and Robbie had shut off the exhibition hall lights. "Hey could you spare a little light, please? I can't see my feet in front of me," Grace said, laughing as she passed through the hall.

"Oh, so sorry. Did I *scare* you?" he said, as he turned on the lights to Hall B.

"Thanks, but you're a little late now. I'm almost there. And no, you didn't scare me, wise guy!" Grace became used to this familiar face. She enjoyed the harmless flirting that occurred between them.

Robbie knew that Grace had been engaged before. But that's all he knew. He remembered when she came into the lobby one night and flashed her diamond ring at him, her face all aglow. He remembered being mildly disappointed when she showed him. But it was different now. She had broken off the engagement well over a year ago. "Too young," she had said. After all, she was only eighteen when he asked her. Her first boyfriend was also her first love. The engagement lasted all of three months. That was all he knew. Grace was a mystery to him. A vivacious, outgoing mystery. How he wanted to let her into his world; include her in his life. If only he could.

"Have a great night, Grace," he whispered slowly.

"Hey, is everything all right, Robbie?" she asked, as she rested her purse and suit jacket on his desk.

"Yeah, yeah. Just wondering what I should do about Kay. It's just not working out. I mean, we've been together for almost a year—maybe even more than that—and I'm just not happy."

Robbie began to tell his story openly, and Grace became enthralled with him.

"Anyway, I don't know. She yells at me a lot. It's like she treats me like a kid. I hate that . . . and she's never happy. She always has something to bitch about! I think she's been cheating on me too. Damn it!" With this, Robbie's features changed. He was becoming furious.

"Well, why do you stay with her then?" Grace asked, inquisitively.

Robbie looked at Grace, and his voice softened. "I don't know. I guess I feel like I deserve her. I mean, she's okay looking . . . not beautiful or anything. But then again, I'm no Joe Handsome either, you know."

"Oh, don't sell yourself short, Robbie. You are a very handsome man. Look at yourself." And with that Grace whipped out the compact from her purse and held his face in her hand. His deep blue eyes shown brightly in the mirror.

"Look at that face," she gleamed. He was handsome. His hair was the color of midnight. His smile was wide and he was six foot-one. He was college educated and charming. She wished he would have more confidence. She wondered why he became so insecure when he talked about his girlfriend.

"Would somebody like you go out with me?" Robbie asked with that coy smile, and for the first time their eyes met. He thought she was beautiful.

"Well, if you didn't have a girlfriend, of course," Grace answered, almost embarrassed that her eyes lingered for longer than a moment. She put the compact back into her purse.

Robbie suddenly took her hand and held it. "Well, what if I broke up with her? Would you go out with me then?"

"Yes, I guess I would," she said thoughtfully, smiling at him. Then he leaned into her and kissed her lips, softly.

"I'm sorry, Grace. I've wanted to do that for so long now that I couldn't help myself."

"That's okay. I just don't want to be the cause of you and Kay's breakup. I mean, if you're going to break up with her, do it because you don't get along or something like that. But don't do it because of me. I mean, you and I may not work out either, and then what'll you do? You've got to do it for yourself." Grace smiled to herself. *Good answer*, she thought.

"You are absolutely right," Robbie said. "But I've thought about this for so long now, it's not sudden to me. It's just that I didn't think you'd actually say 'yes.' Do you know what I mean?"

"I suppose so."

"Well, what are you doing this weekend? Do you want to have dinner?" Robbie asked.

"Sounds like a plan to me," Grace said and picked up her suit jacket and purse. "I've got to go. It's getting late. See you tomorrow."

"Good enough, then," Robbie said with a smile and led her through the front entrance doors.

Chapter 2 - The Locket

The following day Grace arrived as usual, driving down the parking lot at top speed. She'd been warned by the parking attendants before about driving so fast in the parking lot, but she never paid any attention. She pulled in front of the building and ran inside. Late again.

As she came through the double doors, she noticed a woman in Robbie's office. She was five-nine or so, and wore a black leather mini skirt and white button-down blouse. Her makeup covered a seemingly bad complexion. *Kay?* She wondered. But the woman didn't look unhappy, as she was smiling and touching Robbie's arm in a friendly manner. *Couldn't be Kay, who is it?*

As she pulled the sign-in sheet from the outside desk, she heard, ". . . on for next Friday night? Of course!" Grace watched the woman leave the office and glide out the front door, looking back once to wave good-bye to Robbie. Grace saw that he was now standing outside his office, smiling, and when he saw Grace, he looked almost embarrassed.

"Hey Grace, what's up? Ready for the big show tonight?" he asked, trying to conceal his obvious discomfort.

"Hey Robbie, what's up with *you*?" she said, almost mocking him. She was hurt but tried to appear nonchalant.

"Oh her? I study on Friday nights with her," he said casually.

"Sorry. Don't know what came over me. I withdraw that question, okay?"

"Yeah, I see where you might have gotten a different idea. You have nothing to worry about. Look at yourself. You're beautiful," Robbie said coyly.

This man fascinated Grace. She didn't know why. All she knew was that he was charming and appealing. She wanted to get to know him better. She was glad to finally have that opportunity.

They went out that weekend. Robbie took her to dinner and then for a walk along the pier. They talked for hours as they sat on an old bench, watching the seabirds dip into and out of the ocean. She liked him. He was romantic—hopelessly romantic. She liked that. He paid attention to her. It was as if they were the only two people on the pier.

They had been dating for approximately two weeks when they decided to take a drive down the boulevard. It was late November, and two inches of snow had fallen the night before.

Robbie drove a 1984 Pontiac Fiero. It looked like a matchbox car. Grace thought that he looked hysterical when he came to pick her up, all six feet of him getting out of a tiny automobile. Grace liked driving with him. She rested her head on the taupe seat cover and listened as he told her about college.

As they approached the stoplight, Robbie slowed and took Grace's hand. He was smiling. "Waiting for a Star to Fall," by Boy Meets Girl, was playing on the radio. He turned the volume down, and looked at Grace again.

"You are great, Grace," he said. "You make me very happy. I like being with you."

"And I like being with you, too," she said, smiling.

As the light turned green, he noticed a locket around her neck. "Hey," he pointed, "where'd you get that? I never noticed it before. Is it new?"

"Oh, no, it's not new at all. My parents gave me this when I did *Annie* in high school. Remember the play I was telling you about?"

Her parents had given the locket to her during her high school production of *Annie*. She was only a sophomore and to get the lead was quite an accomplishment, considering it was a senior class production. Her parents cut out a picture of her with a curly red wig on, dressed as

Annie, and placed it on one side of the locket. On the opposite side was a miniature picture of the boy who played Daddy Warbucks, also her first love—the man to whom she was once engaged. Grace wore the locket throughout the play, and throughout the rest of her high school years. To Grace, it wasn't just a locket, a piece of jewelry, but a special memory. It was a picture of love from her parents, a picture of remembrance to show her children someday. She never took the locket off at night or in the shower. It became a part of her.

"Yeah, the one you and Dan were in, right? So, who's inside the locket?" he asked almost impatiently, and shifted the car into the left lane.

"Annie and Daddy Warbucks," Grace answered with a laugh in her voice.

Robbie pulled off the road and into the vacant parking lot. "So, why don't you open it then?"

"Sure." Grace opened the locket that was inscribed by her parents, '*To Annie, love Mom and Dad,*' and showed Robbie. "See, don't I look funny in that red wig." Grace started looking closer at the locket, squinting. "Gosh, the faces are so tiny, you can hardly see . . ."

Before she knew it, her left cheek was burning. Robbie had slapped her hard. "Why the *hell* are you wearing a picture of your ex-boyfriend? What, you still love him, is that it?" Robbie's face was red and his eyes were wild.

Before Grace could answer, he snatched the gold chain from her neck, leaving a faint red line on her neck. He twisted the locket until the heart was broken in two and threw it out the window.

Grace tried to stop him, but he kept pushing her away with his right elbow. Afterwards, she just sat there stunned, and then she started to cry. "What's the matter with you? It was a memento from the play!" Grace was now crying harder and holding her stinging face in her hands.

"You shouldn't be wearing things that remind you of your ex-boyfriend, Grace," Robbie argued. "C'mon, you know you're wrong. I don't ever want to see that again.

Understood?" Robbie's face softened as he took her hand, gently.

Grace nodded numbly and turned her face in the direction of the window. She didn't want to argue with him. She sat in the passenger seat confused. *Was she wrong for wearing the locket in front of him?* She wondered, but she didn't think so. And why, when he slapped her, hadn't she jumped out of the car and started walking home?

Grace looked out the window for what seemed an eternity. She finally decided that maybe he was right. After all, Robbie was her boyfriend, not Dan. That was ancient history now. Maybe she should let go once and for all. Turning toward him, she finally spoke. "I'm sorry, Robbie. I didn't mean to upset you, but you didn't have to slap me. Why did you do that?" Grace asked with newly formed tears running down her face.

"I'm sorry, but you really hurt my feelings. If you and I are going to be together as boyfriend and girlfriend, I don't want you wearing things like that. Besides, if you really liked me, it wouldn't bother you to get rid of the locket," Robbie said, as he brushed her tears away.

"Don't ever do that again, Robbie, I mean it," she sobbed, as he pulled her into him. He kissed her face, wiped the few tears that remained, and the argument was over.

Chapter 3 - December 1987

Thanksgiving came and went. Grace and Robbie were fast becoming an item. The weather had turned colder, the nights were becoming shorter, and the two were falling in love. Grace seemingly forgot about the slap that had occurred almost two months ago. She figured he was right. *He* was her boyfriend now. He was the perfect boyfriend. On their one-month anniversary, he brought over flowers and a card that read, "To someone very special, I am falling in love with you."

And now, Christmas was upon them. Sitting beside the brightly lit Christmas tree in Grace's family room, Robbie handed her a box with a large red ribbon around it.

"Oh Robbie, I can't believe you bought this for me! I can't believe you remembered my size and everything!" she exclaimed, as she tore open the Filenes gift box. Inside were a brown suede skirt and jacket, an outfit she had admired weeks ago, but knew she couldn't afford.

"Grace, remember the night we saw that? I went back after I dropped you off and bought it before I forgot your size." He laughed as he helped her try the jacket on.

"You look stunning," he said. Turning to Grace's mother, he grinned. "Mrs. P., doesn't your daughter look absolutely stunning?" Robbie said as he looked again at Grace.

"Yes. Grace, it's beautiful. But Robbie, you can't afford that. You're still in college."

Grace's mother did not approve nor disapprove of their relationship. Because they worked in the same building, she knew Robbie long before Grace had met him. Mrs. Preston became watchful of his comings and goings around the workplace. She used to see various women in his office before, but now, he was dating her daughter. She was concerned. But Grace seemed happy, and he hadn't been disrespectful toward her or her husband, so she accepted him into the family, for now.

* * *

Robbie's family was different. They welcomed Grace with open arms. They thought she was witty and very outgoing. She seemed to get along with his three siblings as well. They enjoyed having her over for dinners and family gatherings. Over the past few months, she almost felt like part of his family.

"Grace, you're so good for Robert. Maybe you can tame him," his mother said one night over dinner.

"What do you mean?" Grace asked innocently.

"Oh, it's just that Robert can get a little defensive sometimes. He and I butt heads a lot, if you haven't already noticed," Mrs. Gagnon added.

Yes, Grace had noticed. Robbie didn't seem to get along with his mother, or his sisters for that matter. She wondered why, but when she asked Robbie, he became angry and told her to mind her own fucking business.

Grace didn't mention it again.

Chapter 4 - 1987-1988

As time passed, Grace's parents started noticing a change in her. She was dressing and wearing her hair differently. Grace's mother, Elizabeth, was five-foot-two. She had dark brown eyes and frosted blond hair. She always wore a tan. Mr. and Mrs. Preston often traveled to Miami to visit her parents during the winter months. To look at her, you wouldn't know she was in her forties. Grace was proud of her mother's appearance. She was a classy woman. She wore designer dresses and suits, carried a Gucci pocketbook and drove a white 1988 Lincoln Town Car.

Grace's father was five-eleven. He had black hair and hazel eyes. Over the years, his slender form had expanded and his black hair displayed a hint of silver, but his eyes never lost their sparkle. Grace remembered seeing their wedding pictures years ago, and recalled how handsome he was. Grace loved hearing about how her parents met.

Jack Preston was in the armed forces in Korea, with another young man named John Connolly. They swiftly became friends and shared stories of home. They talked about how much they missed their families and friends. Months later, Jack received word that his mother was dying and got permission to fly back home to Massachusetts. He spent two weeks by her bedside until she passed away. After the funeral, Jack was preparing to fly back to Korea, when he remembered Johnny telling him that his family only lived ten minutes from his home in Hingham. Jack decided that it would be nice idea to stop by and meet his best friend's family, and let them know that Johnny missed them.

Mr. Connolly answered the door and greeted Jack openly. Johnny had written that Jack's mother was ill, and that he had flown home. Mrs. Connolly, being of Italian heritage, prepared an awesome feast of pasta, meatballs and all the trimmings that go along with an authentic Italian meal. They talked for hours. He felt comfortable with his friend's family. He knew them so well from Johnny's descriptions that he felt almost like a part of this close-knit family.

Johnny had a younger sister, Elizabeth. She was engaged at the time to a marine named Darren, who was stationed in Newfoundland. When Elizabeth walked through the door that day, and down the narrow hall into the kitchen, Jack stood up and smiled. She took his breath away.

Jack flew back to Korea the next day. He told Johnny about the funeral service, and how he had stopped by to visit his family. He asked about Elizabeth. Johnny explained that Elizabeth was engaged to Darren and that they would probably get married within a year or so.

As the days turned to weeks, Jack began to think more and more about Elizabeth and Johnny's family. The next possible leave, he would visit with them again.

And he did. Over the course of three months, Jack and Elizabeth became friends. They listened to Johnny Mathis records. *"Nobody Knows"* became Jack's secret song to her. He wanted to let her know how he felt. He loved her.

Elizabeth became increasingly confused. She was just nineteen years old, and engaged. She thought about how nice Jack was to her and how special he treated her. He showered her with more respect than her fiancé ever did. Darren was a possessive man. He demanded his mother call Elizabeth every night to make sure she was home. Elizabeth was always polite and talked to his mother when she called. Over the past few months, however, it was becoming increasingly difficult.

When Darren came home from Newfoundland, he found Elizabeth waiting at the pier. The next day she returned the ring and explained slowly how she had fallen in love with a man named Jack. She apologized. She cried. Three months later, Jack and Elizabeth became engaged. Six months after that, they were married. They have been married ever since.

Grace's parents rarely argued. They respected each other. And they taught their children to respect themselves also, and raised Grace to be a lady. And now she was wearing miniskirts, tank tops, and high heels.

* * *

"Is Robert telling you how to dress now?" her mother demanded. "And *what* have you done to your hair?"

Grace's light-brown locks were now colored a brassy yellow.

"Robbie likes my hair this color," she growled. "And he likes when I dress like this. What's wrong with it?"

"You don't look like the daughter *I* raised!" her mother barked and stormed off, down the hall, muttering about how he was trying to change her, and becoming like the girls he sleeps with on the side.

Grace heard her and screamed, "You take that back! I cannot believe you just said that."

Mrs. Preston walked back toward her daughter. She decided she would take a calm approach, rather than continue fighting. "Grace," she began, "you just aren't the same girl you were. Look at you. You would never dress like this, or even *think* about coloring your hair."

"Well, I want to be attractive for Robbie. He thinks I look beautiful."

"Grace, you already are beautiful. You are dressing like those girls he flirts with at work. I *see* him. You are better than that . . . you don't have to put up with his behavior."

Grace was aware of her new dressing attire. She didn't much like it either, but she was too ashamed to tell her mother that Robbie *did* make her dress like that.

She, too, had noticed Robbie at work, sometimes talking to a girl, but he always said it was one of the guard's girlfriends or something like that. They were all tall and thin. She had seen redheads, brunettes, and just last week, a blond. This explained her latest dye job.

* * *

One night a few months ago, Grace found a Playboy magazine in his book bag. She had asked him for a pen and he threw the book bag at her. When she found the magazine, she took it out of the bag and questioned him. He denied that it was his, and accused her of being jealous and insecure.

As for Grace and her mother, their relationship hadn't been the same since she and Robbie started dating. Robbie had slowly convinced Grace that her parents were against her and that only he truly loved her. Despite her parents' pleading to break up with him and move on, Grace continued to see him every day. Robbie demanded it.

When they worked together, she would spend her dinner break in his office, watching him work and listening to the stories he told to fellow officers about the thief he apprehended, or the woman's purse he found.

It seemed like whenever he talked, a group would gather to listen. He appeared so charming and self-assured in front of a crowd. Robbie was charismatic and the stories he told were always enhanced by his broad smile and grand gestures. Everybody loved him.

The girls in her office, however, thought differently. They would come in with stories of him flirting in the lobby with one of the models from the show, or that they had seen him in the lounge on his break, flirting with the waitresses.

"Grace, I know you love this guy, but he's a womanizer! Can't you see that? He flirts with everyone!" Margie exclaimed as Grace turned her chair away.

"Margie, knock it off. Just because your boyfriend does it, doesn't mean Robbie does!" She shot her a look that stunned Margie.

Margie and Grace had worked together for over two years now, part-time. Grace liked working with her, but lately, she was becoming very annoying.

"Grace, I've *seen* him," Margie said softly. "I'm not trying to hurt you, and maybe he does really love you, but he's still a big flirt."

When her shift was over, Margie apologized to Grace and asked her to rethink what she said. Grace knew that Robbie was insecure with her, but not to the point where he would openly flirt for attention. She needed reassurance, and after an hour, she decided to call Robbie.

"Oh, Grace, he's not here right now. He's . . . he's in 'D' Hall, I think. Want me to leave a message?" Louie asked, hesitantly. Louie Vitrano had worked as a security guard for over nine years. His hair was gray and his voice was raspy. The guys in security used to call him the 'Godfather.' Grace knew he liked her.

"Uh, no thanks Louie. I'll try back later."

Grace walked quietly down the stairs into the lobby. There was an auto show exhibiting, one with Playboy models and girls in bikinis strutting their stuff on stage. *Anything to sell a car,* she thought. Occasionally, they had a male model or famous actor signing autographs, but Grace never went near them. Robbie didn't like her to talk—or even look at—guys like that.

"They might get the wrong idea," he would tell her. "And I don't want my baby to be with anybody but me."

Sure, over the past year or so, other guys had asked her out, but she wasn't interested. She was happy with Robbie, although once she had snuck down to the lobby to watch the show.

"What the hell are you doing!" he yelled. "Checking out the guys . . . is that it?"

"No, Robbie," she replied. "It's just that I hardly ever get to see the show. I'm always on the switchboard."

Robbie grabbed her arm hard, and led her up to her office. His fellow security officers looked on, but said and did nothing. Grace was embarrassed.

"What did you do that for?" she asked. "You made me look like a fool!"

"Shut up. *You* were the one who made *me* look like a fool. How do you think I feel when I see the girl *I love* gawking at some guy?" He slammed the door behind him, locking it from the outside.

"Hey, unlock the door! R-O-B-B-I-E!" she hollered, as his footsteps became farther away. "Robbie!" Grace sat on the steps and started crying. This was becoming too familiar.

As Grace remembered that incident, she flinched. How she hated recalling those bad times. He kept telling her how much he loved her, over and over again. He told her how much he wanted to marry her someday. If only she could stop being so insecure and trust him. He didn't like reprimanding her like that, but she had to learn that he only loved *her*. She made him angry.

Grace suddenly felt silly, sneaking around the hall, checking up on him. *What am I doing, anyway?* she thought. As she turned to go back to her office, she heard laughter. It was now ten-thirty and the show had ended a half an hour ago.

"Oh, Robbie . . . you are so funny. Then what happened?"

Grace recognized the voice. It was Dotty, a waitress from the lounge. Dotty was five-foot six, had short bottle-blond hair and blue eyes. *Probably colored contacts,* Grace guessed. She wore stretch jeans and an off-the-shoulder sweater, revealing freckled shoulders. Grace had seen Robbie talking to her in his office before, but just assumed she was signing in or out. She trusted Robbie.

The laughter now rose. Grace's stomach began to twist. Her palms were sweating. *Why was she doing this? She didn't believe Margie, did she?*

"So, are we still on for tomorrow night, babe?" Dotty whispered, as her left hand stroked the back of his head.

Just then Grace felt her insides explode. Her face was flushed, her hands were wet, and her stomach was churning. She felt sick. She stopped for a moment to compose herself and then walked right up to the pair.

"Hi, Honey. I tried to call you earlier, but Louie said you were here. Oh, Hi Dotty. Anyway, I didn't know if you've had a chance to have dinner, but I have some pizza upstairs for you, if you want it." *Good,* she thought. *I didn't appear too upset. Pretty calm, actually.*

"Oh, he already had dinner, Grace. I fed him in the lounge, earlier." Dotty smiled.

"Yeah, I already ate. Um . . . you ready to go?" Robbie asked, as he nervously put his arm around her.

"Yes," Grace said, thinking of what Margie had told her.

The next day Grace called in sick to both jobs. She wanted to think about things. She spent the day in her room, reading over cards and letters from Robbie. Over the past year, she had put together a photo album. It included the card from their first week anniversary, the napkin from the little Italian restaurant where he had taken her on their one-month anniversary, and many other remembrances of their relationship. As she flipped slowly from page to page, her thoughts of him became more and more powerful.

She came across some rose petals and a card that read: "I love you, Babe! Love, Robbie."

She recalled that night when he gave her those roses. She was working upstairs, answering the switchboard. The boss at her full-time job had just given her a raise. She couldn't wait until it was time to go home, so she could tell Robbie all about it on the ride home.

As she stood up to turn the office lights off, she heard music from outside the window. Her switchboard overlooked 'B' Hall, where some of the shows were exhibited. But this night, there wasn't a show.

As she looked out the window, she saw Robbie standing alone in the middle of the hall. He had on his traditional white cotton shirt, gray polyester pants and blue sport coat. He had peach roses in his hand and on the ground, a radio played *"Brown Eyed Girl"* by Van Morrison. A yellow forklift stood close by with what appeared to be a picnic basket and candles on it. He had shut the hall lights off and the candles glowed beautifully in the darkness.

Grace ran down the stairs and into the hall. "Oh, Robbie! I can't believe you did this. This is so romantic," Grace said, as a tear rolled down her face. "Nobody has ever done something like this for me before!"

"Your chariot awaits, my dear," he proudly stated, as he pointed to the forklift. They spent hours in that hall. They talked about the raise she got and they drank sparkling apple cider until it was time to leave. When he brought her back to the lobby on the forklift, he jumped off first, and extended his hand to help her down. As he kissed it, he whispered how much he needed her.

He really loves me, Grace thought, as she recalled that night fondly. She closed the book, happy again, and fell asleep.

Chapter 5 - August 1988

"Well, I can't believe it's taken so long for us to get together," Mrs. Gagnon said, as she reached for the pitcher of lemonade. Mrs. Gagnon had decided one-week prior that maybe the parents should meet. Mrs. Preston was a little hesitant, but agreed, for Grace's sake.

"Yes, I know," said Mrs. Preston. "Thank you for inviting Jack and me over. You have a lovely home."

"Well, if you got it, flaunt it," she said with an arrogant laugh. Robert's mother, Sarah, was a nurse. Her husband, Rob Sr., was a Certified Public Accountant and Harvard graduate. They lived in a Garrison Colonial, light gray with black shutters. The front hedges were perfectly trimmed and a deck of concrete surrounded the massive built-in pool. A gray cabana was set off to the back of the yard, encased with beautiful oak trees. It seemed so peaceful.

A golden retriever wandered lazily around, sniffing the ground for scents of leftover burgers and potato salad. The patio furniture was white wicker, with pale pink and yellow floral print pillows on every chair.

Grace's house looked somewhat like this. Except for the backyard, they lived in the same type home. Grace's father had put in an above ground pool a few years back, with a large deck surrounding it. She loved her house.

Grace's parents couldn't afford to go to college, but Elizabeth was now the General Manager of the company where Grace worked part-time. Her father was a Property Claims Manager for a large insurance company. Grace was proud of them both.

Sarah took Grace's mother around the house for a tour, while Grace and Robbie's father walked around the front, examining the shrubbery.

Grace was sitting by the pool when Sarah and Elizabeth walked through the gate. They found a spot in the shade and Sarah began, "So Grace, when are you going to join my son at college?"

"Oh, I've been thinking about it lately. I really like my job, though," Grace said, smiling as Robbie walked over and sat beside her.

"Well, you know, Grace, if you don't go to college, Robbie will eventually outgrow you. You won't be smart enough for him."

Grace was shocked. Her face turned stark white and her stomach started to knot. She felt tears building up and quickly excused herself. She had to walk around the length of the pool, through the gate surrounding the pool, and into the cabana. *God, I hope I don't start to cry right now,* she thought. *Why does this pool have to be so big?*

"Grace, wait!" Robbie yelled, but she was already inside. "Mom, you're such a bitch. Look what you've done. I can't believe you just said that!" he yelled.

"Neither can I," Mrs. Preston said, and got up to see if Grace was okay. *God, I can't stand this family,* she thought as she passed the gate. *Bunch of snobs.*

As she entered the cabana, Mrs. Preston came up behind her daughter and put her hand on Grace's shoulder. Grace flinched.

"Oh sorry, Mom. I didn't know it was you," she sobbed as she reached for her mother's hand. "Can you believe she said that to me just now?"

"C'mon Honey. You dry those tears and get right back out there. You'll never be outgrown by that parasite. You're smarter than him *right now*. Any fool can see that."

"Mom, please don't pick on Robbie. It's his mother we're mad at. Let's just go home," said Grace, and with that, the two emerged from the cabana.

Robert Sr. and Grace's father were still out in the front yard when they saw Grace through the fence, running past.

"What was that all about?" Jack asked as they walked through the gate and into the pool area.

"Oh, I merely stated that Grace should go to college," Sarah explained. "I just worded it incorrectly, that's all. She is so very bright and she has so much to offer . . . she could become so much more, if she went to school."

"Well," Jack replied, "we're proud of Grace no matter what she does. She's not ready right now. When she is, she'll go, but it will be *her* decision." Then he added, "Look at Elizabeth and me—neither one of us went to college and we're doing fine."

"Yes, well . . ." Mrs. Gagnon glanced disapprovingly as she looked him over. She turned her head and walked away.

"Well, Honey," Jack said, as he turned to his wife, "you all set?"

"Yes, let me just grab my pocketbook," Elizabeth replied, as she picked it up from the table and walked around the pool toward the gate.

"Well, thank you for having us over, Sarah. You have a lovely home," Mrs. Preston said. Despite her anger, she remained refined.

"Yes, well, you'll have to come back again, when you can stay longer," Sarah responded.

"Grace, you coming?" Mr. Preston hollered from the other end of the pool.

"Mr. Preston, I would like to talk to Grace for a while, if you don't mind. I'll have her home in a few hours," Robbie replied, before letting Grace respond.

Grace's parents waved good-bye and drove down the street. Grace watched the taillights as they faded in the afternoon sun.

Robbie waited for his parents to go into the house, and then he pulled Grace behind the house, beneath the enclosed porch. They heard his mother above, closing the porch windows. She had just turned on the central air conditioning. Robbie listened and waited for his parents to walk from the porch and into the family room. "How *dare* you embarrass me by running in the cabana like a damned little child?" he barked.

"Robbie, I thought you were on my side," Grace said. "Your mother was dead wrong, saying something like that to me—especially in front of my parents. What nerve!" Grace was fuming. *I will not take the blame for this one,* she thought.

"Don't answer me back," Robbie said in a low tone, and slapped Grace across the face. She immediately put her hand on her left cheek and sat down slowly on the cement steps leading into the downstairs cellar.

"Robbie! What's the matter with you?" she asked, as tears formed and rolled down her face.

"I'm tired of you. You're nothing but a baby. You are so damned spoiled, it makes me sick. Why don't you G-R-O-W up?" Robbie taunted her for a few minutes and then grabbed her pocketbook that was laying next to her on the stairs. He started running with it toward the pool.

"Robbie, knock it off. C'mon, give it back," Grace cried, as he laughed and ran around the pool.

"What's the matter, *baby*?" he laughed, as he watched her chase him. Just then, Robbie jumped into the pool with her pocketbook. He held it over his head and began to tease her. "C'mon in Grace. Water's warm. C'mon and get your pocketbook."

Grace had never liked the water. She didn't mind floating once in a while on a raft, as long as nobody tipped it over, but she didn't like the idea of going under water. As a little girl, her Uncle Ralphie had picked her up and tossed her into the ocean. He had three kids of his own and they loved the water. When he did it to them, they screamed for more. The water was no more than three feet deep, but Grace was only five years old, and frightened. She couldn't breathe. She felt the water fill her lungs and she started screaming. Grace had never liked the water since then.

"Robbie, I'm not coming in. Just put my pocketbook on the edge, please. Don't make me beg." Grace started to walk closer to the edge of the pool, and closer to Robbie. "Why are you doing this?" she asked.

"Oh, look," Robbie said, as he started to open her pocketbook, "an address book." Robbie was obviously displeased upon opening it because he threw it into the deep end of the pool and started swearing furiously. "Why do you have guys' numbers in there, you pig?" His voice started to rise, and Grace was scared.

"Robbie, no!" Grace started to yell, but the book found itself at the bottom of the pool. "Why do you have to be so insecure? Why?" Grace sobbed, as she moved closer to Robbie. He was now toward the middle of the pool.

"You're right, Grace. I'm sorry. Here, you can have your pocketbook back," Robbie said, as he glided toward her.

Grace walked over and knelt down by the cement edge, being careful not to get too close.

"Here you go," Robbie said, as he held up the pocketbook and leaned in her direction. "I didn't even get it wet." He laughed.

Just as Grace reached for the strap of the pocketbook, Robbie pulled it back and Grace was caught off balance. She fell into the water face first, and began to sink to the bottom of the ten-foot pool. When she reached the bottom, she pushed with her legs against the bottom of the pool as hard as she could, sending her soaring back to the top. She let out a gasp and began to choke on the water in her lungs. Then she started to cry.

"Robbie . . . you know how afraid I am of the water. Why did you do this?" And with that, Grace started to swim toward the shallow end of the pool. Robbie, however, didn't let her go that easily.

"Oh, Robbie is the big jerk, huh? Why am I always to blame?" he said, as he took her arm and squeezed tightly. "You're afraid of the water? Well, the only way to get over those fears is to jump right in," he said with a mad laugh.

Before Grace knew what was happening, Robbie grabbed her hair and pushed her under the water. She struggled and kicked, but he held her down. Grace thought she was going to drown. Just then, Robbie's mother opened the window to the porch.

"Robert, what the hell is going on out there?" she yelled.

Robbie let go of Grace's hair, and she bounced back up to the surface.

"Oh nothing, Mom. Just playing around," he laughed. His mother closed the window just as Grace began to cough and choke.

"Let this be a lesson to you, bitch! Don't ever fucking embarrass me like that again," he said, as he pushed her head under the water one last time, and got out of the pool.

Chapter 6 - December 1988

Christmas was upon them once again. Mrs. Preston had asked Robbie's parents to join them this year, since it appeared to her that this relationship Grace had with their son just wouldn't die. When they accepted, she made a sign of the cross, and asked God to give her the strength she needed to get through the night.

Grace's house was breathtaking. The shrubs out front were covered in white lights and each window had one light glowing from inside. Holly covered the lamppost and a decorative wreath hung from the front door. The snow had fallen a few nights before, blanketing the ground below.

Inside, the oak railing, which led from the foyer to the second floor, displayed a green garland. On the stereo, Robert Goulet could be heard singing, *"This Christmas, I Spend With You."* It was one of Grace's favorite Christmas songs. She remembered as a child of four or five that her mother would dress her in red velvet, put on the Robert Goulet album, and baste the ham while she waited for the family to arrive.

Four stockings hung from the upstairs fireplace—stockings that Grace's great-grandmother had crocheted before she passed away many years ago. They were green, red and white with each name sewn at the top. Each year the stockings became heavier and heavier, until gifts were left on the fireplace ledge, as well as inside the stockings. Grace's parents were very generous. It was obvious they adored their children.

As children, Grace and her older brother, Richard, would run to those stockings and dump them out all over the plush beige carpet. Her mother would make homemade hot chocolate, and her father would sneak into the kitchen for some leftover ham. Grace's brother was now a college graduate and working as an engineer for some high-tech company outside of Boston. Grace was so proud of him. Of course, he wasn't at all like her. He was extremely book smart, very quiet and reserved. As they got older, she grew to admire those qualities.

Now, sitting in the living room and remembering by the crackling fire, Grace turned to Robbie as he took her hand. "Grace, I want to give you something this Christmas. Something that is very special to me and a few other people," Robbie said, a quiver in his voice. He waited while she opened the Christmas card he had bought for her.

"No matter what it is, I'm sure I'll love it, Honey," Grace replied. Opening the card, she began to cry. The words spoke of love and forever, of future and happiness. Robbie had written a poem on the left side of the card, declaring his unending love for her. He wrote how sorry he had been for incidents in the past and hoped that tonight would start the beginning of a new relationship. "C'mon downstairs, my dear. Your gift awaits."

Robbie asked her to close her eyes, as he led her down the first flight of stairs and into the foyer, where he then asked her to open her eyes. Before her stood a beautiful oak hope chest, wrapped in plastic.

"Oh, Robbie," she squealed, as she flew down the stairs. "This is beautiful. Oh my God, I love it."

"Open the wrapping, Hon. You're in for a surprise," Robbie said. With that, Grace's father pushed through the crowd of family and friends, to see his daughter's reaction as she read the inscription from her dad. *"This chest was made with a lot of love, for my baby girl. Love, Dad."*

"Dad? You made this for me? You did this?" Grace cried and hugged her father tightly. The hope chest was so beautiful. The seat cover was a peach and beige flowered fabric. Those were her favorite colors. She thought it was the most beautiful thing she had ever seen.

"Yeah, Honey. Do you like it?" Her father wiped away the tears in his daughter's eyes, as well as his own. He loved her so much. She was his baby girl, and tonight, she was becoming a woman.

"Oh, Dad, Robbie . . . thank you both so much! I love you guys."

From this point on, Grace's life would never be the same.

PART II - THE UNRAVELING

CHAPTER 7 - JANUARY 1989

As the month passed, Grace thought hard about the incident in August with Robbie's mom. She wanted Robbie to be proud of her. Maybe Robbie really would outgrow her. She was smart, but maybe she should go to college.

"We could be together every day, Grace," Robbie explained, as they discussed the idea. "I could walk you to class . . . we could have lunch together . . . it would be so great. Will ya think about it, baby?"

So she did. She thought hard. On January 9, 1989, Grace would become a freshman.

However, the night before the big day she was over at Robbie's house chatting with his parents about her excitement and nervousness about college, when she got a terrible, shooting pain in her back. She couldn't stand up, and her stomach started burning.

"Oh my God! This can't happen. Not now," she cried.

"I'm taking you to the hospital," Robbie said, grabbing her coat and putting it around her shoulders. "Let's go."

They reached the hospital quickly. Entering the emergency room, she saw doctors swarming around in white coats and hospital pants. It was late, and she thought that her parents would want to know what was happening.

"Call my parents," Grace said, as a nurse lifted her into a wheelchair.

"Yeah, okay," he replied.

She waited an hour to be seen, and finally, a nurse arrived with what appeared to be a moving bed. She wheeled her into a room, the size of her bathroom at home. It smelled like disinfectant and urine. *God, I hate hospitals,* she thought.

She spotted her parents outside and called to them. "In here," she said.

Her mother heard her, tugged her husband's arm, and followed the voice.

"Oh, Honey, what happened?" Her mother had been crying. Grace didn't understand why.

"Mom, I'm okay. It just hurts a lot," she answered. "Why are you crying?"

Turning toward Robbie, she said, "Would you mind getting me some tea?"

Grace's father interjected that he would go, and after the look that he got from his wife, it was decided that they would both go. After the door closed behind them, Grace's mother began, "Honey, you can tell me the truth. Did *he* do this to you? You can tell me. We'll *help* you." By now, Grace's mother was wiping away tears, while Grace stared blankly at her.

"God! *No,* Mom! I think I might have some type of kidney infection . . . at least that's what I heard one of the doctors say earlier." Then she continued, "What would *ever* give you the idea that Robbie would hit me?"

"Honey, you've become a different person since you two started dating. You dress differently, you dye your hair all the time, and you've become withdrawn. You don't even have any friends. I don't like to see this happening to you."

"No, Mom, Robbie didn't do anything, okay. Can we drop it?" Grace lay back and rested her head against the pillow. They sat in silence until the two men arrived.

Meanwhile, two hours had passed. Soon after, one of the specialists on call determined that she did have a kidney infection and would need to stay the night on an IV.

"Mom, I start school tomorrow. I have to go," Grace sobbed. She had waited for so long to make this decision and now it was being taken away from her.

"Honey, listen to the doctor. You have an infection. You can't possibly go to school tomorrow." Grace's mother felt bad, but knew she couldn't make it to college the following day.

"Mom, I want to do this. Please," she begged.

"Okay fine. I'll talk to the doctor and see if you can come home. They'll probably put you on antibiotics or something, and you may feel sick tomorrow. Do you still want to go?" Mrs. Preston's voice softened.

"Of course," Grace responded, with tears in her eyes. She had never wanted anything more.

Thirty minutes later, Grace's mother and father entered her room.

"Okay, get your stuff, you're coming home," her father said. "But you have to come back tomorrow after school for additional testing. Promise me you will?"

"Oh yes, yes. Thank you so much, you guys." Grace smiled. Her back still hurt and the IV made her feel nauseous, but she didn't care. She would start college tomorrow.

The next morning she got ready for her big day. She wore the new jeans and pink sweater her mother had given her, with matching 1-inch Nine West shoes.

When Robbie came to pick her up, she was standing on the front steps. She wanted so much for him to be proud of her. He pulled in the driveway and jumped out of the car almost before it had fully stopped.

"What the *hell* are you wearing?" he snapped.

Grace looked down and noticed the pumps. "Sorry, should I wear flats?" she asked dejectedly.

"How many times have I told you, I don't want you dressing like this in front of anyone. Those jeans are too tight." As he yelled, he pushed her against the wrought iron railing, causing her to fall on the brick steps. Her new jeans ripped.

"So you want other guys to notice you today, is that it?" He then started walking over toward the car and told her to go in and get changed. When she came out, she had on baggy pants, a black turtleneck, and sneakers. She grew to hate those sneakers. This would become her attire throughout college.

They didn't speak on the way to school. She was hurt, her knee was aching and her stomach was in knots again. They arrived at school at 8:45 A.M. and he walked her to class.

"Okay, now, sit in the front row so I won't have to wait for you to come out. I have classes to take too, you know. And don't let me see you take that jacket off. I can't believe you wore a turtleneck without something over it."

"Why? It's not too tight or anything. And since I had to get changed, I didn't have time to find a sweater to wear," Grace replied, as she secretly prayed he would just leave.

"Well, just don't let me catch you without your coat on. Guys will be staring at your breasts, and I don't want to have to protect your honor on your first day of class." He then kissed her forehead and walked down the hall.

About a half-hour later, Grace noticed the room was growing hotter. She was feeling a little squeamish because of the antibiotics, and decided to take her jacket off. *Class is almost over anyway,* she thought.

Ten minutes later, the door opened a crack and there stood Robbie, watching her. He had gotten out of class early to walk her to her next class. When he saw her without her coat on, he became furious. She saw him, and immediately felt sick. *Oh God,* she thought, *please don't embarrass me.* Too late. He opened the door completely, walked in and grabbed Grace's book bag.

"There's been an emergency," he said to the professor, as he dragged her out by her arm, slamming the door behind them. Before she could speak, he punched her across the left side of her face. Her nose started to bleed and her lip quickly swelled. It was as if someone had hit her with a heavy rock.

"What did I do?" she cried, looking frantically in her purse for a napkin so the people in the halls wouldn't take notice. But people did. Her left eye was bloodshot and her lip swelled up immediately.

"I *told* you not to take off your jacket. What? . . . Did you think I was kidding?" he yelled, while dragging her into the elevator, and back to the car.

Robbie seemed to enjoy this public display, dragging her outside by her arm, like a scolded child. He knew that Grace wouldn't raise her voice, because she didn't want people to stare. She didn't want to cause a scene.

"Clean yourself up. You look disgusting," he said, laughing, as he opened the car door and threw her inside. He then brushed himself off, checked himself in the rearview mirror, and went back to his classes.

Grace felt weak.

"What am I going to do?" she said to herself, as she looked at her face in the compact—the same compact she had used when she and Robbie first kissed. It seemed like so long ago. Grace reapplied her makeup, added a touch of lipstick to her swollen lip, and went back to her remaining three classes.

Later that afternoon, Robbie met her at the car, as if nothing had happened. Her bottom lip was swollen and her nose was still stinging. She got into the car slowly, and waited for him to speak. Grace was scared.

"How were your classes, Grace?" he asked inquisitively. "Meet anyone new and exciting?" He was amusing himself. She wondered where he was going with this.

"Fine. I have an English class that I think I'll really like," she said softly, as they drove out of the parking lot.

As they started for home, she felt nauseous again. She stopped listening as Robbie accused her of flirting with the guy in her English class, and she tuned him out. She wanted to go home and forget this day ever happened.

"Are you listening to me? *Look* at me when I talk to you!" he screeched. Robbie then started accusing her of thinking she was too good for him now that she was in college. He began to slap her left arm, waiting for a reaction, as if he wanted her to fight back.

"Will you just leave me alone?" she begged. "I feel like I'm going to be sick. Can you drive a little faster?"

"Oh, I feel like I'm gonna be sick. Can you drive a little faster?" He mocked her. "Sure," he laughed as he poked her stomach, "anything for the little baby."

This time when he raised his hand again, Grace blocked it with her left arm. When she did, he got angry and punched her hard in the stomach. "Robbie, stop the car. I'm gonna be sick," Grace cried, as he pulled over.

"Don't get sick in my car," he growled. As she opened the car door, she vomited.

The next week she had to stay home from college. A girl who worked for her mother went to class for her and took notes until she was feeling better. The doctor's report stated that the kidney had ruptured.

Chapter 8 - The Workplace

Grace thought that college would be a great release—an outlet for her to meet new people and maybe become a little more independent from Robbie. She knew that the relationship was heading for a terrible fall, and had confronted Robbie on several occasions.

"Robbie, why do you have to get so angry at me?" she questioned, as they sat in his office and ate the Chinese food she brought in on her night off. "Don't you trust me?"

"No, it's *you* who doesn't trust *me*. You're so insecure . . . and besides that, we're always together," he snapped.

"Well, if that's the problem, why don't we stop seeing each other every day?" she responded, thinking that she was finally getting somewhere with this.

"Oh, why? Do you want to date somebody else?" Robbie barked.

"No, I just don't want you to hurt me anymore, and I'm trying to figure out why you do . . . I love you so much, Robbie. I mean, I know you tell me that you love me all the time, but then I'll find some Playboy magazine in with your school books, or some 900 number written down somewhere. I know you'll deny it and tell me that the stupid magazine isn't yours and you tell me that you don't call the numbers, but my gut instinct is telling me that you're lying, and I'm beginning to wonder why I put up with this."

There, I said it, she thought. She started to take a mouthful of Egg Foo Yong, when she felt something wet and sticky drip from the top of her head onto her shoulders.

She looked up at Robbie, who had just poured duck sauce over her head and all over her new white blouse.

She felt her hair. Clumps of brown were burying themselves into the roots. Security officers were sitting outside his office, curious as to what was going on. But nobody said anything.

Grace started crying in a muffled tone, not wanting the guards to hear her. "What did you do that for?" she panted.

"You want to know why you put *up* with this? I'll tell you why, you little whore!" he growled in a low voice, as he threw the plates on the floor. Robbie grabbed her arm and continued to speak in a whispering, vicious tone. "Because you will always be a low life fucking l-o-s-e-r! You couldn't even make your relationship work with your first boyfriend. *He* was smart! He knew you were a stupid, ugly piece of shit. Why do you think he's engaged now? He smartened up! I, on the other hand—I try to be good to you, to treat you nice, and buy you things, and you have the nerve to say you don't *deserve* this?"

A few minutes had passed, and the guards had walked away. Grace's hair was sticky and her eyes were red. She was sweating and her face was tear-stained. She sank to the hard cement floor as he ridiculed her, and she couldn't seem to move.

"Pick this shit up, you pig!" he yelled, as he threw the remains of the dinner on her lap, and walked out, laughing.

She grabbed the napkins on the desk and began to wipe up the mess. She was crying softly now, rehashing the hurtful words he had just spoken. When she finished, she went into the ladies room, wiped off her stained blouse, and tried to remove the clumps of brown in her hair.

As she came out of the ladies room with her eyes still wet, Robbie was standing before her. Grace flinched.

"I'm going home," she said defiantly, as she walked toward his office to get her things.

"Oh no you're not. You and I are going upstairs," he said as he grabbed her by the hair.

Grace knew what this meant.

The executive offices on the second level were equipped with sofas. Eleven offices were on that floor, and

Robbie had the key to all of them. Grace had seen the sofas on occasion when Robbie felt so inclined. She knew how he hurt her and did unspeakable things to her upstairs.

* * *

The very first time he raped her, it was after a fight when he caught her in the lobby watching the show. After he locked her in the office, he waited until the show closed. He made sure all the guards had gone home, except Willy. Willy worked in the West Lobby, and they communicated by radio only. Robbie wouldn't have a problem with him.

He unlocked the door to the office where he left her, and walked with her toward the lobby. She had nothing to say. She was upset, and knew that should she start an argument, she would be the loser again.

Entering the lobby, he walked over to the executive offices' main door and told her to follow. He had some flowers and a card upstairs. He wanted to apologize. Grace felt relieved. No fight. She entered one of the offices where a dozen roses in a crystal vase and red ribbon were prominently displayed. The card with the flowers said, "I love you baby, I'm sorry." There was a bottle of wine and some strawberries too.

"Thanks Robbie. This is all really sweet. I can't believe you went out of your way like this," she gleamed. "I love you."

"Yeah, well I love you, too . . . So let's have a drink and make up, okay," he said as he pulled the wine off the oak desk.

"No thanks, Honey. I'm actually kind of tired, and I have to work again tomorrow. Can we do it tomorrow night instead?" she asked.

He slapped her face, and squealed, "You little ingrate! I do all this for *you* and you don't even *fucking* appreciate it? No, I don't want to do this tomorrow—I want to do it now, do you understand me?" Robbie shut the door behind him, and locked it.

Grace noticed and, for a moment, became frightened.

"No, Honey, I just want to be able to fully enjoy our time together. I have to work tomorrow and I don't want to rush tonight," she said, trying to appear calm.

"We are going to celebrate *tonight*!" Robbie snapped, and grabbed at her blouse. He fumbled for the buttons and became impatient, causing three or four to fall carelessly to the floor. Her jeans were next. As he scratched her thighs with his fingernails, she began to bleed.

"Robbie, you don't need to do this. C'mon, I don't *want* to."

Grace was still a virgin. When she had started dating Dan, she was only fifteen. They dated for over a year before they realized that they were in love. Dan asked Grace when they would make love, but Grace wanted to wait. She was only sixteen and a half by then. Six months later, Dan went into the army and when he returned, they got engaged. They never made love. Now, Grace was frightened. She didn't want her *first time* to be like this.

"You are my girlfriend, Grace. You belong to me. Nobody else can have you like this." As Robbie tried to free her breasts from the encasing brassiere, Grace started to scream.

"Robbie, STOP IT! You're hurting me!"

Grace kicked and hollered but he held his palm over her mouth and slapped her when she bit him. She kicked at him and her body thrashed from side to side.

"Oh, you wanna play hard ball, huh?" he laughed, as he reached for the wine bottle. Dumping the contents into the neatly lined trash barrel, while his hand muffled Grace's cries, Robbie held up the empty bottle. Grace was still trying to get him off her, but this only seemed to excite him. "Yeah, you like it rough . . ." he said with eyes gleaming. As he plunged the bottle into her, Grace felt a burning sensation. It was tearing, ripping her insides. Blood spewed onto the beige carpet. Grace screamed. She was bleeding and her face was sore.

"Who do you love?" he asked as he leaned into her, with droplets of his sweat piercing her skin.

She didn't answer.

"Who do you *fucking love?*" he demanded.

"You, Robbie," she sobbed, and turned her face toward the bookshelf. She concentrated on the dust balls collecting underneath it.

When he was through with her, he pushed her over with his foot and spat on her naked and quivering body.

"If you ever mention this to anyone, I'll *kill* you," he said, in words that chilled. "You are dirty now. Nobody will ever have you, except me. You need me, Grace. You belong to me." Robbie then picked up the bloodied bottle and tossed it into the garbage.

"You should *thank* me for loving you."

* * *

It all came flooding back to her now, as he dragged her upstairs, yet again.

"C'mon, be a good girl and I won't hurt you," Robbie said, as he opened the door to the CEO's office. "You like this, don't you? Didn't you and ole Danny boy play like this?" When she didn't answer, Robbie snapped at her, "Get on the floor!" as he began to unbutton his pants.

"Robbie, no! Please just leave me alone. I won't make you mad anymore! I'm sorry."

Grace cried. Her head was pounding. Between her hair being yanked and the headache she had, she could barely hold her head up. The duck sauce had dried, and her hair was sticky. She just wanted to go home.

"Oh, you're s-o-r-r-y! You are my girlfriend!" he yelled as he knelt down on top of her.

He tried to kiss her lips and when she turned her head, he hit her hard against her cheek. "Don't you *ever* turn your face like that again!" he shouted.

Grace's nose began to bleed and her right eye was stinging. As he entered her, he called out a name—it wasn't hers. For over an hour, he kept her on the floor. After he finished with her, he went into the men's room to clean himself off.

Chapter 9 - Dan

Daniel Dennis McKay had been Grace's first boyfriend. They met in the garden at the local high school in Scituate. Grace was practicing a solo for the spring concert and he was listening from the library, six floors above. When he heard her melodic voice, he put his history book on the old wooden table, and looked outside.

There, standing below, was Grace, a girl of fifteen. She wore a pale yellow dress and white sandals. She was holding a sheet of music in her right hand and blocking the sun with her left.

He stood watching and listening to her until the bell rang. Class was over for the day. He saw the girl start to gather her books and called down to her.

"Hey!" he yelled, "Wait up! I'll be right down."

As Grace looked toward the direction of the voice, she realized he had been yelling to her. Suddenly flattered, she smiled up at him and nodded.

A few minutes passed, then Grace spotted him running from the hall into the garden.

"Hi," he said. "I heard you singing. You were really, uh . . . great!" Dan said bashfully.

"Thank you," Grace replied.

"Hey, where are you taking off in such a hurry? School's over," Dan questioned, as he took in her soft scent and gold-brown eyes.

"I'm going to try out for the chorus in 'Annie'," Grace said, as she walked toward the auditorium.

"Oh yeah? Sounds pretty interesting," Dan said with a smile.

"Well, I'm only a sophomore, so I can't try out for any leads . . . I don't think," Grace said, as they entered the auditorium hall.

When they reached the entrance doors, she turned to him. "Thanks for walking with me," she said. Then, "Thanks for saying I sang well, too," Grace said as she shook his hand.

"Well, . . . I guess I'll let you go. I hope I'll see you around again." And with that, he walked away.

Oh nuts, I didn't ask his name! she said to herself. *Probably too old for me anyway. Looks like a senior.*

Grace tried out for the chorus that day, and the director, also the English teacher, Mrs. Smith, called her back for a second audition. She had to read lines this time.

"But, I thought that if you wanted a chorus part, you wouldn't have to read?" Grace asked the director, curiously.

"Well, we think you'd be good for the lead. You know . . . *Annie.*" Mrs. Smith laughed and handed her the script.

Grace nervously read from Act II, Scene VI, and was told that they would let her know in a few weeks.

"Oh my God! Grace, come here quick!" said Diane. Diane was Grace's longtime friend and confidant. Diane was the one who pushed Grace into trying out for the chorus in the first place. She was standing in front of the auditorium looking at what appeared to be the casting sheet.

"Did you get a part?" Grace asked, as she stood on her tiptoes to see above Di's red locks.

"No, but you did! Look!" she shrieked.

Diane moved out of the way, and stood beside Grace. She took Grace's hand and lifted it to the top of the page. It read:

The part of Orphan Annie: Grace Preston
The part of Daddy Warbucks: Danny McKay
Other cast members:...

"Oh wow!" Grace exclaimed. "I can't believe it! I've got to go home and tell my parents!"

Grace practically flew home that day. After all, she was only a sophomore and she had been given the lead in a Senior Class Play!

I wonder who Danny McKay is, she thought, as she neared her street.

Grace talked to her family that night and they too couldn't believe it. They knew she liked to sing, but act too?

The following day after school, Grace stopped by the auditorium to find out when rehearsals began. *Oh, there's that guy!* she thought, noticing the boy from the garden.

Grace walked down the narrow aisle leading to the stage. "Hi again! Long time, no see," she flirted.

"Yeah. How are you?" he said.

"G-r-e-a-t! Remember the play I was trying out for?"

He nodded, coyly.

"Well, I got the lead! I'm Annie!" She was smiling and her arms were waving in the air.

"*You* are Grace Preston?" he asked. Then added, "I was wondering who was gonna play the lead with me."

Grace looked at him inquisitively, and then it hit her. "No way! You're Daddy Warbucks . . . I mean, Danny McKay?" she asked, obviously pleased with this news.

"Yeah. Nice to meet ya . . . officially."

As afternoon rehearsals turned into late night get-togethers, Grace and Danny became closer. On December 29, 1984, he asked her to be his steady girlfriend. She had never been happier.

* * *

After their four-year relationship, engagement and now, close friendship, it was Dan whom she called when Robbie left her stranded somewhere, bloodied and bruised. It was Dan who came to pick her up, clean her face, and help her regain her strength to go home.

"Oh Danny, thank you for coming. I'm sorry . . . I know your girlfriend probably hates me, but I can't call my mom and dad." She sobbed frantically, as he brushed her hair from her eyes.

"Grace, I'm, gonna *kill* this guy! I swear!" Dan hated to see her this way. She was so fragile, so sweet. He wondered how this monster could get away with this.

"Danny, you have to *promise* that you won't say or do anything! You don't understand, he'll *kill* me . . . He's made threats before . . . Please Danny, don't!" Grace was becoming hysterical. She knew Robbie's wrath. He had already threatened to kill her if she told anyone. She was taking a chance in even calling Dan.

He sat without saying a word for ten minutes, then said, "Grace, please let me help you. Tell me what I can do?" Dan was almost to tears as he spoke. He still loved her—obviously, he still loved her.

"Just be my friend. I don't like you to see me like this, but I can't go home all bloody and ugly," Grace cried.

"You are *not* ugly. You're so beautiful, Grace. God, I want to *do* something!"

Dan was defeated. He made a promise to her that he would be her friend. She seemed so terrified that Robbie would kill her if anybody knew. What could he do?

Chapter 10 - The College Years

Robbie began walking Grace to and from every class, to make sure nobody talked to her. He became ever more obsessed. After class one day, Grace stopped to pick up the school newspaper at the information booth in Wheatly Hall. She had just aced an exam and felt pretty good. Her professor let the class out a few minutes early, so she had some time to kill before Robbie would be by to meet her. A classmate appeared next to her at the booth. Timmy—well, that's what she heard his friends call him—was tall with blond hair and hazel eyes. And he was handsome.

"Hi. I saw you leave class after you got your exam back. How'd you do?" he said, smiling. Grace was scared. If any one of Robbie's friends saw her talking to this boy, she would be dead.

"Good," she responded flatly. "Got an A minus."

"Wow, I got a C. Do you think maybe we could study together sometime?" he asked.

"No. I'm sorry, but I really have to go."

Grace walked away quickly before anyone saw her. As she came to the stairwell, she felt a hard blow from behind, causing her to fall down five steps. It was Robbie.

"You little slut! Did you think I wouldn't see you flirting with that guy?" Robbie kicked her as she tried to get up. "Stay on the floor— that's where you belong!" He then spit on her, spraying her hair and face.

"What . . . do you actually think that guy could like a two-bit whore like *you*?" he laughed. "You'll never get away from me!"

Grace couldn't go to the rest of her classes. She was a mess. Robbie told her that he would take her to his house, because *her* family didn't want her around. Once they got into the car, he started to fight all over again.

"Robbie, please stop this. It's insane," she cried. "I love *you*. I'm not interested in meeting anybody else. Please believe me."

"Shut up!" he argued. "You just love rubbing it in my face that guys think you're attractive, don't you?"

"No, I don't even look at anyone else. I walk with my head *down*, back and forth to class so that no one will talk to me . . . Today, somebody asked me why I walk with my head down?" she cried.

"Oh, and I suppose it was a guy who asked you, right? . . . RIGHT?" Robbie was furious. "Answer me, you damn little whore!" As he yelled, he grabbed her hair and pulled so hard that clumps of blond hair stuck between his fingers. He shook them off, disgusted, and they fell on her lap.

"Please Robbie, stop yelling!" Grace kept crying, and was holding her head in her hands, aware of the recent bald spot. She started crying louder, almost uncontrollable.

"Shut up, will you! I'm tired of hearing you bawl like a baby!" he yelled, and stopped the car. They were about two miles away from her house.

"Get out!" Robbie demanded, and pushed her with his right hand onto the gravel below. Before she could get up, he was gone.

Chapter 11 - The History

Grace and Robbie had dated for almost two years now. She hated what she had become. She hated living in fear every day. When she tried to break up with him, another fight would ensue and he would threaten to kill her. Her self-esteem was literally demolished. She suffered from vaginal bruising and abdominal pain on a regular basis. Her parents became increasingly worried about her. She had become a recluse. After they left for work in the mornings, she would leave, and come home long after they fell asleep. It was easier this way.

She became adept in the artistry of applying makeup to cover bruises and scratches. She wore clothes that covered the other various imperfections. Robbie's parents witnessed the arguments but never interfered.

"You two have to work this out by yourselves," Mrs. Gagnon would say.

In between the periods of abuse, Robbie would spend extravagantly on her, showering her with roses, cards and chocolate. He bought her necklaces and bracelets. He wanted Grace to change, telling her that he didn't like to hit her, but she provoked him. He told her that he had never struck another girl before and that it was Grace who had a problem with insecurity, not him.

Meanwhile, Grace was spending a fortune on stereo equipment, bomber jackets, a CD player and all his favorite CD's—anything to make his abuse less frequent. She thought that if she bought him some of his favorite things, then he would see how much she loved him. The gifts seduced him for a few days, or even a week here and there, but the abuse always continued.

Grace was utterly terrified.

* * *

One day after school, she and Robbie were studying in the family room of his house. His parents were working and he wouldn't let Grace call her parents.

Grace missed her family. She missed the closeness she had once shared with them. She was a shadow of her former self now, a humble, frightened little girl, wishing she could tell her parents all the horrible things he had done to her. But how could they understand? They never had to deal with any major issues like this.

Grace squelched the tears that began to form as she thought about her parents, and instead concentrated on her studies. About an hour or so passed, and Robbie was becoming increasingly angry. Grace could sense it, but she didn't question him. She didn't even look at him.

"Grace, what are you reading?" he asked, as he sat on the rust-colored leather sofa and tapped his right foot impatiently on the thin gray carpet.

"I'm studying for tomorrow's exam. It's in my law class. We're learning about Hitler and all the things he used to do. God, he was a horrible man . . . Did you know," she continued, "that he had the SS men tie the shoelaces of the prisoners together, so that after they were gassed, they would have a pair of shoes to sell?"

"Wow! You really are becoming smart, aren't you?" Robbie said, in a tone that made Grace shiver. "Can I see your book?"

"Why?" Grace asked, hesitantly.

"Because, Babe, I want to read about the Jews, okay?"

Robbie took the heavy textbook and began to flip through the pages. Then he noticed a piece of white lined paper with someone's number written on it. He held it up and threw it in her face, while tossing her book to the floor.

"Who is Jerry Hines, Grace?" he shrieked, yanking the yellow highlighter from her hand, as he pulled her off the chair.

"Jerry is the girl I study with before this class. You know that. You walk me to the McCormick Lounge every Tuesday and Thursday," Grace responded calmly. *Not again—not tonight,* she thought.

He tore the paper into tiny bits and pieces, and quickly picked up the law book.

"Looks like you're gonna have to study without a book from now on, huh!" Robbie tore the pages out one by one, and as Grace grabbed for it, he slapped and kicked her legs and chest, until she dropped to the floor in defeat.

When he finished pulling apart the book, she crawled beneath him and tried to recover some pages. She sat for a long while completely numb. All her emotions were used up. She had nothing left. Suddenly, Grace remembered the diary. Should she still have it, she would write how she would commit suicide tonight—explain to her family how sorry she was, how unhappy she had become . . . but she didn't have the strength.

Chapter 12 - Grace's Diary

Grace kept a diary of everything that had ever occurred to her since the age of five years old. She wrote about her new dress that her mother bought her for the third grade. She wrote about her crush on Michael MacNamara in the fourth grade, and the purple dress she wore when he actually walked her home from school one day.

She wrote about her dreams and wishes as a little girl, to grow up and marry a prince, like she saw in Cinderella. How she wanted to wear that dress and meet that prince.

As she grew older, she wrote about boys—every boy she had ever known. The first kiss: Timmy. The first unescorted dance: Jimmy. Her first boyfriend: Danny.

Danny took up most of her diary. They dated for four years, and he had a right to belong in it. They shared romantic walks and picnics, studied in the school cafeteria together and rehearsed for countless plays in the auditorium. She remembered when he asked her to be his girlfriend on December 29, 1984. She was just 15 years old. He was seventeen. Danny was a handsome boy—five-eleven, with brown hair and hazel eyes. He had a grin that could make the dead smile. Yes, she had loved him, truly loved him.

Diary, guess what? He asked me! Can you believe it? It was in front of my entire family. He's such a ham! He had my uncle record it on video while he asked me!

He disguised it in a boot box. One of those work boot kind of boxes, ya know? Anyway, I

> *opened it up, and there was a beautiful white Gund teddy bear, with a ring box (opened), to show a gorgeous one-carrot (oops) karat, diamond. (Marquise).*
>
> *He wants us to get married next year . . . what do you think? I don't know . . . we'll talk about it. Gotta go, he's waiting.*

Grace didn't write about Robbie. She preferred to leave that part of her life to herself. She didn't want anyone to know about the bruises, and especially the rapes. Nobody would believe her. Robbie was too convincing. And besides, what if Robbie ever saw it!

One afternoon, however, Grace's mother requested that she be at home for dinner.

"Yes, if it means that much to you, Robbie can stay too!" her mother shouted.

As the women prepared the meal and set the table, Grace called for Robbie. She wanted him to see the chocolate cake her mom had made. When she called him, she heard a noise coming from her room.

"Robbie, is that you? Come here, I want to show you the great cake . . ." Grace's mouth dropped when she saw Robbie sitting at her desk and reading her diary, while flipping through pictures of Dan and her.

"Why do you still have these?" he shouted, as he tore the pictures up in front of her. "And why am I not mentioned anywhere in here?" He shook the diary in her face, and shut her bedroom door.

"You and I are going to take a little walk before dinner, understood?" he whispered, as he pinched her arm.

"Why?" Grace asked. "We're eating in just a few minutes." She felt as if she was going to cry, but didn't want her family to see, or hear her.

"C'mon. Get your jacket. Tell your folks that we'll be right back . . . GO!" he barked. Robbie stuck the diary in his coat pocket as he walked down the hall into the living room. He grabbed some matches off the fireplace.

"Mrs. P., Grace and I are going to take a quick walk before dinner, okay?" Robbie asked as he opened the front door.

"Uh . . . that's fine. Just be back in about ten minutes or so," Elizabeth said from the kitchen. She watched him close the door behind them.

"Where are we going?" Grace asked as he led her away from her house.

"Oh, we don't need to go far. Follow me," he said with a sinister chuckle. He dragged Grace by her right arm to the end of the dead end street, where a narrow brook led to the old wooden fort that Grace and her brother used to play in. He told her to sit.

"I don't like this, Robbie. What are you doing?"

Robbie pulled out her diary. "You are going to *burn* this right here . . . right now," he said.

"I am not! That is my life . . ."

Grace jumped up and started to rebel, but Robbie grabbed her neck with his right hand so tightly, she thought she would pass out. Then, he kicked her genitalia and she fell to the ground. He pulled her back up by her neck, squeezing tight.

Realizing that he couldn't light the match while holding her neck, he reached with his left hand into his jacket pocket. Remembering the red Bic lighter that the Playboy *Playmate of the Month* was passing out during the most recent show, he retrieved it from his pocket and forced it into Grace's hand. He demanded she hold it while he held the diary above it. She couldn't scream; she could barely breathe.

All she could do was watch her memories go up in smoke.

Chapter 13 - The Engagement

With each passing day, Grace became ever more frightened. She tried to concentrate on her studies, but whenever she did, Robbie got angry. *She wasn't paying attention to him,* he would say. And he would again punish her.

School became increasingly difficult. She was constantly bruised and sore, her genitals were tender, and she hadn't been able to have a full night's sleep for months.

It was November 1989; Grace had just taken her last final before school ended for Christmas break. Robbie met her after class with a dozen peach roses. The girls in her class "oohed" and "aahed" over the flowers, while Grace wondered what he was up to this time.

"Darling," he said, "these are for you."

"Thank you, Robbie," Grace said softly. "What are they for?"

"Babe, it's our two-year anniversary today. Don't tell me you forgot?" he mused as he took her books and handed her the roses. "We are celebrating tonight. It's our two year anniversary and you just aced another final, right?" he asked.

Robbie was in great spirits. He was acting as affectionate and loving as he had when they first met. For a moment, she hoped . . . prayed. Yes, maybe he had finally changed.

That night, Grace dressed in a festive red angora sweater and long black skirt. Her hair was auburn now. She applied her makeup, curled her hair, and waited patiently for Robbie to arrive.

"Mom, do *you* know where we're going tonight?" she asked.

"Honey, all I know is that he's taking you somewhere nice for your anniversary. He seems to be really happy lately, don't you think?" Elizabeth had noticed that Robbie was acting differently. At least he and Grace hadn't fought for a few weeks, anyway. She prayed that maybe he was finally growing up.

* * *

Robbie arrived on schedule at seven o'clock. He left the car running while he rang the doorbell. Over the past year or so, he and Grace had purchased a car together. Robbie thought it would be easier than having two, when they were always together anyway. Grace was hesitant, but finally agreed.

"You look stunning," Robbie said, as he looked at her from the foyer. She was standing atop the stairs.

"Thanks, Robbie. So do you," she said. Robbie had on black slacks, a white dress shirt and red sweater. They looked like twins. They looked, for once, like a couple in love.

"We are going for a special dinner. I hope you're hungry," Robbie said, as he helped her with her coat.

Grace had to laugh. When she met Robbie, she had weighed one hundred and twenty-one pounds. Over the past two years, she had lost nineteen pounds. She always had a great appetite. Her mother used to say that she could eat as much as her father. But since meeting Robbie, she was flustered and nervous all the time. She rarely ate when her mother cooked and usually threw up if she ate after she and Robbie had a fight. Whatever the reason for the weight loss, Robbie liked her thin.

"Yes, I'm starving," she lied.

They reached the restaurant, only five or so miles from Grace's house. La Bella was known for its romantic atmosphere and great Italian cuisine. The hostess seated them at the corner table with a window view of the lake, now frozen over and covered with snow.

On the table a kerosene lamp burned brightly. The tablecloth was mauve. The napkins were white. She would always remember tonight.

The waiter came over to the two who were holding hands, and excused himself. He took their orders, and vanished promptly, as he smiled and said something in Italian.

*   *   *

"Well, here we are," Robbie began. "I can't believe we've been together for two whole years. That's a long time, huh?"

"Yes, it is." Grace smiled. "This is a beautiful restaurant, Robbie. Thank you for bringing me here tonight. Just like old times, huh?"

"That's what I wanted to talk to you about, Grace. I've thought about you a lot over the past few weeks, and I know I've been mean to you in the past. I thought about how much you must love me to put up with me, and how much I love you," Robbie continued, watching Grace's expression.

"So, I wanted to start fresh . . . I know I've said that before, but I mean it now. I love you, Grace—so much. I'm sorry for the things I've done to you, but it's only because I love you."

Grace didn't say a word. She listened as he went on about how much he loved her, and needed her, and she began to feel sorry for him. He seemed to be sincere about all the things he was saying. He was still holding her hand.

Their dinner arrived and they shared a glass of wine as they ate. "To a life of unending happiness with the woman I love," Robbie said, as he raised his glass to hers.

When they finished eating, Grace and Robbie sat for another thirty minutes and talked. She was really enjoying tonight. He helped her out of the chair, helped with her coat, and then walked her to the car. As she got into the car, Robbie took her hand.

"Baby, for our anniversary I put together something that I'd love for you to hear. Just give me a minute to drive to the lake, okay?"

Grace sat there wondering what was going on. Had he totally changed? What had happened? She decided not to question it.

Robbie drove to the lake across the street as the snow began to fall. He popped a tape in the car stereo and turned up the volume. Grace heard Robbie's voice:

> *To Grace on our two-year anniversary. I'm giving you this tape on our anniversary with the hopes that all our dreams together will never die. You've made me very happy over the past two years and I love you for that, Grace. I hope these two years are only a small portion of the life we'll have together.*
>
> *Love Always, Robert*

Grace was beginning to cry, as she looked over at Robbie, who was also crying.

"Wait, there's more," Robbie said, turning up the volume again. This time, Grace heard music, the beginning of a song. The words caught Grace by surprise:

> *No more talk of darkness, forget these wide-eyed fears, I'm here, nothing can harm you, my words will warm and calm you.*
>
> *Let me be your shelter, let day light dry your tears. I'm here, with you, beside you, to guard you and to guide you.*
>
> *Say you'll love me every winter morning. Turn my head with talk of summertime. Say you'll share with me one love, one lifetime.*
>
> *Anywhere you go, let me go too.*
>
> *That's all I ask of you . . .*

Grace was shocked. Did he really feel this way after all that had happened? Yes, he had changed. Things would be different now.

Grace was crying. This time the tears were tears of joy. She noticed Robbie was crying, too, openly. He hugged her and kissed her for what seemed like forever.

"Grace," Robbie said weakly, as he rewound the song, "please listen to the song again, okay?"

"Okay, Honey, that was so beautiful. Thank you so much!" Grace gleamed between tears.

As the music started playing again, Grace noticed that Robbie was holding something in his hand. She looked closer as he presented it.

"Grace, I love you with all my heart and soul. Will you . . . will you marry me?" Robbie asked, choking back the tears.

The diamond was marquise cut. He slipped it over her finger and kissed her hand. It must have been a karat and a half! *How it sparkled!*

"Oh, Robbie, I don't know what to say." Grace cried, as she looked at the beautiful ring on her finger. "You've done such horrible things to me. You've made me feel dirty. You scare me." Grace watched Robbie's expression. He was still crying.

"I know I can't take back the past, Grace. But I promise to go to counseling or something. I don't mean to hurt you. Sometimes, I get so afraid of losing you, that I act crazy. I don't want anyone else to look at you. I can't bear the thought of losing you, you know?" Robbie was holding Grace's hand hard, almost pleading with her to accept his proposal.

"I'm afraid, Robbie. I'm afraid you are going to hurt me so badly one day that I'll die." It was the first time Grace had ever voiced her ultimate fear.

Robbie's eyes flew wide, and he grabbed her into his chest, holding her close. "Oh my God, Grace. No! I love you!" Robbie stroked her hair and pleaded with her to give him another chance.

"Robbie, accepting this ring changes everything. It says we are starting a future together. It says we are making that commitment to love one another forever." Grace's words were muffled in his chest.

Robbie moved her away from him, and touched her face gently. "Grace, I love you. I will do whatever it takes to make you happy for the rest of my life. I swear!"

Grace looked down at the ring on her finger, and sat silently for another few minutes.

Finally, Robbie spoke up. "Just wear it for a while. Think about it, okay? You'll see." He smiled.

Grace agreed, thinking he must truly love her. And he *had* changed. From now on things were going to be great!

Chapter 14 - The Reaction

Back at Grace's house, everyone waited. Robbie had suggested that his parents be at the house when he and Grace returned from dinner. Mrs. Preston had also invited her parents.

Grace's mother tried to appear happy before the two went for dinner. And now, it was all crashing down on her.

She was scared for her daughter. She saw the way Grace jumped when somebody touched her, remembering the incident in the cabana. Also, she hated the way Grace waited for Robbie to finish speaking so as not to interrupt him. Mrs. Preston watched as her daughter become a shell of her former self over the past two years, and there was nothing she could do.

Grace's father was a quiet man. He was the epitome of a *nice guy*, never one to yell or scream. He didn't know how to talk about things like relationships with his daughter, letting his wife do that. All he knew was that when he met her mother, they dated, they fell in love and got married. They never fought. He never called her names or told her how to dress.

"Jack, I'm worried about Grace," Elizabeth said just after the two had left for their big dinner.

"Honey, Grace is just going through a phase. She's not sure who she is, so she's trying out different styles and stuff like that. Don't worry, she'll grow out of it," he said, as he patted her head and kissed her forehead.

"No, Jack. I mean *Robbie*. I know he's hurting her and there's nothing I can do. If I bring it up to her, she denies it and grows closer to him. If I don't bring it up, it tears me to pieces. Jack, I just see her lying dead on a street corner somewhere, and she won't let me do anything to stop it!"

Elizabeth started crying. She was tired of pretending. She was tired of acting as if she liked Robbie and his family; tired of inviting him and his parents over for dinner and holidays. And now, Robbie and Grace were getting engaged.

* * *

At eight-thirty, Robbie's parents arrived with a bottle of champagne.

"So, it looks like we're going to be related," Rob Sr. laughed, as he handed the champagne to Elizabeth.

"Please, come in," Elizabeth said, ignoring his remark.

They sat for an hour or so chatting about work, the weather, their kids. Then suddenly the door opened.

"Congratulations!" Sarah blurted out, before they had even walked down the stairs.

Elizabeth ran up the stairs and met them halfway. She hugged her daughter hard. "I love you, Honey" she said, and took her coat.

Grace and Robbie sat on the sofa chatting endlessly about their plans, while Grace's parents entertained his mother and father. Robbie's father proposed a toast to the young couple, while Grace's father got everything on video.

She looks so happy, he thought. *Maybe Robbie has changed.*

CHAPTER 15 - THE ACCIDENT

Three days had passed since the two became engaged. The girls who worked at Mrs. Preston's office were hounding her to have Grace come in and show off the ring. Grace had taken a week off to enjoy some time with Robbie, and just take a break. Classes were over for six weeks, and she could finally relax.

"I promise, Mom, I'll come in tomorrow and show off the ring. Robbie and I are going out tonight though, so it'll have to wait another twelve hours. Okay?" She laughed, as she kissed her mother on the cheek.

Robbie had planned on taking Grace out for dinner and then to see a movie. They hadn't fought in weeks, and Grace was beginning to fall in love again.

She heard the familiar honking of the horn. Robbie was right on time.

"See ya later, Mom. Tell Dad I said 'bye,' too," Grace yelled from the foyer. As she reached for the door, her mother stopped her.

"Grace, it's December second. There is snow outside. Why are you wearing a miniskirt and heels?" she asked, as she pointed at her.

"Oh Mom, don't start. I'm late. Robbie's been outside for at least five minutes."

"Well, he can wait while you get changed. Go on . . ." she said impatiently.

Grace opened the door, and mouthed 'wait a second' and then hurried up the stairs and down the hall into her bedroom.

Grace knew this was Robbie's favorite outfit. She had on a black ruffled miniskirt, black stockings and heels. She wore a mint green off-the-shoulder top with long sleeves. It showed off her now blond-again hair.

She threw on a pair of pants over her skirt and threw on a sweatshirt. It would be easy to take off in the car.

"Okay . . . I really gotta go, Mom," Grace said, as she opened the front door.

"Let me see . . . much better . . . see you later. Don't be home too late," she called as her Grace got into the car.

Robbie took Grace to Starbucks, a jack-of-all-trades type of restaurant. It was casual and convenient to the movie theater located inside the mall. They ate quickly, realizing the time, and rushed off to the movie. *Internal Affairs* was playing, with Richard Gere. Something about a cop gone bad.

"Thanks for dinner, Robbie," Grace said, taking his hand

"Thanks for coming," he smiled.

They were sitting on the left side of the theater. Robbie had the aisle seat, and Grace sat to his right. She turned her head to the back of the theater when she heard some kids laughing. Then, something caught her eye.

To the right of her was a man who looked remarkably like Danny. It had been a while since she had spoken with him. He was engaged, after all, and she didn't think it fair to bother him with her problems. She wondered if he knew she was engaged. Her eyes lingered on the man long enough for him to look back and smile. *Oh no!* She thought.

The next thing Grace felt was a blow to her stomach. She felt the wind knocked out of her, and she couldn't breathe. She bent over, holding her stomach. When she could speak, she turned to Robbie and said quietly, "Honey, I know why you did that, but I wasn't looking at him. It's just that he reminded me of Danny," she whispered, almost desperately, so others wouldn't hear. She wanted to cry.

"You haven't changed, you whore!" Robbie said with disgust in his voice.

Grace looked around at the people surrounding them. She smiled nervously.

"Robbie, please don't yell," she whispered. "We can talk about it later."

"No way. You can get your own ride home, you little slut! Why don't you go *screw* that guy? That'll get you a ride home." Robbie finished his speech, pinched Grace's left thigh, stood up and walked out.

Grace sat stunned for a few minutes. The lights had gone out and the movie started to play. Grace was too afraid to look behind her. She knew people were watching. She decided to watch the movie, because Robbie had done this before. He'd get mad, walk out, and end up sitting ten or so rows behind her until the movie ended.

As the lights came up, she felt someone tap her left shoulder.

"Excuse me . . . I saw that guy you were with . . . he left about twenty minutes ago. Sorry." It was a woman from two rows back.

Grace was truly embarrassed. She got up wearily. Her thigh was pounding and her stomach hurt. When she got outside, she started crying. She walked toward the parking lot where Robbie was probably waiting in the car.

When she got to the parking space, she was frantic. It was close to midnight, bitterly cold and the wind had picked up. The car was gone. Grace ran back to the mall entrance, hoping to go in and use the phone. She knew it was late, but her father would pick her up. Suddenly, she saw the high beams of Robbie's car gleaming in her direction.

Grace was sure he was going to hit her, so she dropped to the ground. The pavement was cold and wet. Her stocking ripped, and she skinned her left hand. She caught a glimpse of the diamond, sparkling in the night.

Robbie pulled the car next to her, rolled down the window and spat at her.

"Look at you. You're pitiful! Get in the car."

Grace pulled herself up and walked quietly to the passenger side door. As she reached for the handle, he started to speed.

"Ha, ha . . . what's the matter, Grace, can't open the door?" Robbie laughed as she ran alongside the car, crying and panting. Her hair was soaking wet and her hand was still bleeding from scraping it.

After a few minutes, he stopped the car. Grace got in, humiliated. She was also very angry.

"How *dare* you treat me this way? What is *wrong* with you?" Grace snapped. Before Robbie could see it coming, she slapped him hard across his face. It was the first time she had ever done that.

Slapping him was the worst mistake of her life.

Robbie's face exploded. He looked like a mad man. In an instant, he pushed her hard against the passenger door, slamming her head against the cold window. Then he punched her face with his right hand while trying to steer the car with his left, until her nose and mouth started to bleed.

"You son of a BITCH!" he fumed. "You just fucked up, do you know that? You just fucked up!" As he yelled, his face turned purple. His eyes were wild and she could barely recognize him.

Grace tried to defend herself by blocking his punches with her hands, but to no avail. She felt the blood drip from her mouth and onto her neck. As she tried to wipe it away, another blow would cause another steady stream. He was pulling her hair and yanking her head back and forth until she sank into the space below the glove compartment.

"Get up, you filthy pig!" Robbie yelled, as he grabbed at her blouse. "Who do you think you are? You are nothing but an ugly, stupid slut! I don't even want to marry you! What was I thinking?"

As Robbie lunged for her blouse, he ripped it. Then he started to scratch her breasts, leaving traces of bloody fingernail marks on her.

"God, Robert, NO! Please . . . stop . . . I can't . . . breathe . . ." Grace whimpered, as she put her arms over her breasts. "I can't take it anymore . . . please . . ."

But Robbie didn't stop. He punched her hard across the face and spit at her. She tasted it on her lip and wiped it away. She was weak and couldn't defend herself anymore.

As he neared her house, he pulled the car behind her old high school. He got out of the car and walked over to the passenger side door, opening it quickly.

"Get out of the car!" he yelled.

When she did not respond, he dragged her out by the roots of her hair, and threw her onto the cement sidewalk.

Got to get up! she thought to herself. *Got to run . . .* But she couldn't move. Her face was bloody and soaked with stinging tears. She had bruises on her breasts, thighs, arms and legs. She was lifeless.

She heard Robbie muttering something about her being a "piece of . . . worthless . . ." and her mind went blank. The next thing she heard was Robbie pants unzipping.

"Oh, God. No! Please! Don't do this!" she heard herself crying and felt her body trying to move, but couldn't.

She felt something enter her. It felt narrow and icy cold. She felt her insides sting and then burn and she heard herself cry out in pain.

"You like this, don't you! Tell me you like it, you worthless piece of shit!" he said, as he thrust the object deeper.

"Did *Dan* do it to you like this? Huh?"

Grace closed her eyes and prayed he would just kill her. It would be better than living like this. She thought of her childhood, her house, and the little dog she used to have . . . anything to block out what was happening.

He proceeded to masturbate on her breasts, while he forced the object inside of her. When he was finished, she heard him toss something aside. It sounded like a piece of metal. It was. He had used a small pipe that was lying in the dirt, to rape her.

As she tried to sit up and pull her skirt down, he kicked her vagina. "I'm not done with you, whore!" he yelled. He held her body down with his left foot, and spit on her. Her legs were sticky and her skirt was soaked. She reeked of semen and blood. As she dragged herself up, she vomited.

Chapter 16 - The Aftermath

When he dropped her off, she hid in the garage for a few minutes. It was almost three-thirty in the morning. She knew her parents were sleeping, but she couldn't go into the house crying. They would hear her.

Grace composed herself and went into the house. She went immediately toward the downstairs bathroom where she took off all her clothes and threw them in the trash. She hadn't looked at herself in the mirror yet, but she knew it was bad.

Taking a face towel from the closet, she ran water in the sink, and finally looked up at the vanity mirror.

Grace flinched. She couldn't recognize her face. "Oh God . . . what is happening to me?" she whispered, as she touched the glass in disbelief.

She dabbed her face lightly, to wash off the dirt and blood. Her left eye was red from the broken blood vessels. Her nose was scratched and bloody. The perfectly lined lips were swollen and grotesquely purple. A blood blister appeared on her bottom lip.

She examined herself slowly, trying not to scream in shock. Her hair was in clumps and she could actually see bald spots. Bloody traces of fingernail markings were on her neck. As she stood in front of the full-length mirror behind the bathroom door, she flinched again, and then moved closer.

She touched her breasts softly. *God that hurts,* she thought as she washed the dried blood out of the deep lacerations. *I hope this doesn't leave a scar.* She had welts on both arms from where she had tried to block his punches, bruises on her legs and stomach, and her vagina was caked with dried blood. *How am I going to cover this up?* she wondered.

After she washed the blood and semen off, she took a garbage bag from underneath the sink, and filled it with her clothes, ripped stockings and heels. She opened the back door and tossed the bag into the trashcan behind her father's tool shed. She was only wearing a peach towel that barely covered her body, and her bare feet were now stinging from the cold. She came back inside. It was four-thirty-seven A.M. Climbing the stairs, she stumbled down the hall, and into her room. She closed the door behind her. She would fix her face tomorrow.

Chapter 17 - The Realization

The next morning after Grace's parents went to work, she got up and slowly limped into the bathroom. She turned to shut the door and caught her reflection.

"Oh my God!" she screamed. "NO! No, I can't take it anymore! I can't! I can't . . ." As Grace cried, she looked back at the mirror. "Damn you, Robert! *Damn* you!" And with that, Grace punched the reflection in the mirror over and over again, until it shattered.

After a while, Grace stood, picked up the broken pieces of glass off the floor, and threw them into the garbage. She touched her face again, recalling how just yesterday she had looked *normal. This is never going to heal,* she thought, as she examined her lips, her breasts . . . .

What would she say to her mother? She was supposed to go in the office today and show off her diamond. *We've only been engaged for four days!* As she wandered slowly back into her room, a terrible thought occurred to her. She realized that eventually Robbie would indeed kill her.

As Grace showered, she looked at her breasts. The scratches were deep and she knew that eventually they would become scars. From experience, she knew the bruises would heal. Her face, on the other hand, was a mess. She needed to come up with an explanation. A fall? An accident—yes, a car accident. She would tell her mother that she and Robbie were in an accident. The specifics would come later.

"Breathe deeply . . . be calm . . . an accident, that's all," Grace repeated as she grabbed the keys and headed for the door. As she started to open it, someone was opening it from the other side. She let go. It was Robbie.

"Oh my God!" he shrieked, and turned his head.

"What's the matter, Robbie? You can't bear to look at what you've done? Are you happy now? You've turned me into a freak!" Grace started crying. The makeup she had so carefully applied began to melt, and the bruises became more apparent.

"Baby, I am *sorry!* I didn't think I did this . . ."

"Robbie, I've got to go to work now, and tell everyone that I was in an accident! All because of your insecurity! What the hell is wrong with me!" she continued. "I can't believe I let you do this to me? You are sick!" Grace couldn't believe what was pouring out of her mouth. She suddenly became frightened that he would hit her again, and quickly put her hands above her face.

Robbie started clapping, slowly at first and then faster and louder. "Put your hands down. You're such an actress! You belong on stage with your loser boyfriend, Dan!" Robbie then turned and walked out, slamming the door behind him.

Chapter 18 - Mom's Reaction

Grace walked through the lobby, and up the stairs. *Whew! Nobody noticed*, she thought. Maybe she did a better makeup job than she thought.

As she opened the door to her mother's office, she heard the footsteps running back and forth upstairs. She knew the girls were anxious to see her 'beautiful' diamond.

"She's here!"

Grace heard her mother yell as she climbed the last stair. And then she saw her.

"Oh, no!" Mrs. Preston gasped, as she covered her hand to her mouth. "What happened to you? Are you all right?"

"Yes, Mom. I just . . . Robbie and I got into a little accident after the movie last night." Grace watched as her mother began to cry. She shut the door to her office, so that the girls couldn't hear her.

"Did *he* do this to you? Damn it, Grace, tell me the truth!" Grace's mother began to dial her husband at the office. "I'll have your father go over there right now! Where is he?"

"Mom," Grace cried. "No, I was . . . we were driving home last night, and as we started to get off at the Scituate exit, a guy in front of us slowed, because of the slippery roads. I jammed on the brakes and we ended in a snow bank. I hit my head on the steering wheel," Grace finished. *Sounded like a good story*, she thought.

"Why were *you* driving?" Grace's mother asked, as she put the phone down.

"Because Robbie was . . . tired. He drove the whole way up . . . and that was forty-five minutes. Plus, watching a movie can make you tired, too. I wasn't that tired, so I offered to drive back." Grace was almost proud of herself. She had become quite skilled at lying to her family and friends over the past two years.

"Grace, if I ever find out that he did this to you, so help me God, I'll kill him myself!" She was crying and yelling all at once. She walked over to Grace and hugged her tightly. "I love you so much, Honey. You need to know that. I know Robbie has you convinced that your father and I don't love you, but we do. We would do anything for you!"

"Mom, I was in a car accident, I swear!" Grace cried. She wanted to tell her mother right here and now about everything, but she was in too deep. Where would she begin? Grace's mother wiped her eyes and slowly opened the office door, where hungry faces were waiting to see her ring. When they saw Grace, they too, shirked away. She had to explain what happened all over again, and hoped the story was the same.

CHAPTER 19 - THE RING

The following day Robbie stopped by to tell Grace that he had to go back to the jewelers to have her ring appraised. He explained that he hadn't already done it because he was so eager to give it to her. They had only been engaged for five days.

"Robbie, why don't you go? I'm still sore and honestly, it hurts to even walk," Grace said softly.

"Spare me the acting job, okay? You are not going to make me feel guilty, so just shut up," Robbie said, as he walked down the stairs into the foyer. "Now, c'mon. You have to go anyway."

Grace put her head down and walked with him to the car. She had yet to drive this car that *they* had bought.

When they arrived at DeScenza Diamonds, a jewelry store in Boston, a tall man with a firm brow and silver hair awaited. Mr. Hawthorn was his name.

"Mr. Gagnon, thank you for coming. Now, as you know, there are a few . . . Dear, were you in an accident?" he interrupted himself, staring at Grace.

Grace, obviously embarrassed, replied, "Yes, just two nights ago. I'm okay, though."

"Oh, that's just awful! Well, at least you're okay. Now, where was I? Oh yes. Now, as you know, there are a few details for us to go over regarding to the lady's ring," he said, pointing to Grace, who had just sat in a crushed velvet emerald chair, next to an encasement of wedding bands.

"If you'll follow me," he said, as he led the two through the store and into the back of the room, where a large gray metal door, covered with bars, awaited.

"Looks like a vault," Grace whispered to herself, as he stood in front of her.

Mr. Hawthorn heard and began to laugh quietly, as if she amused him. "Why yes, Miss Preston. This is where all the diamonds are kept. Security purposes and whatnot, you know," he said, as he turned the heavy circular handle two or three times until it popped.

"Right this way," he said, pointing to a rather plush corner office.

The three sat. Robbie and Grace sat on the two high-backed chairs before a large mahogany desk, where Mr. Hawthorn began to shuffle some papers.

"Miss Preston, I must say . . . it is very rare that a bride-to-be offers to pay *half* for her engagement ring. But, whereas Robert here is still in college, I think it's rather nice." Then he added, "Robert, you've got a great girl here."

Grace's mouth dropped. She sat up, moved closer to the desk and glanced at the paperwork. *Oh, this can't be happening!* she thought.

She glared at Robbie. As she turned away, she felt his hand appear on her thigh. He patted her twice, and then pinched her hard. *Damn him!*

"Mr. Hawthorn, will you excuse Robbie and me for just a brief moment, please," Grace said, as she rose from her chair. She felt faint.

"Of course. Of course. Take your time. I'll still be here," he said in a friendly manner.

She and Robbie left the room and found a vacant office two doors down. She shut the door behind them.

"What is going on here?" Grace demanded. "Where do you get off telling me that I'm paying for half this ring—which, by the way, means absolutely nothing to me!" Grace hadn't noticed that she was now yelling.

Robbie slapped her face. "S-h-u-t up!" he demanded. "You think *I* could afford a seven thousand-dollar ring? You must be out of your mind! No, you are going to put half on your Visa. You can pay it in installments and you won't say a word."

As he turned to open the door, Grace said, "Why then did you even ask me? It's obvious this isn't working out—just look at me. Do you think I want to spend the rest of my life looking like *this?*" Grace said, as she pointed to her face.

"Go to hell," Robbie said and walked out.

He wandered back into Mr. Hawthorn's office, and within a few minutes, Grace followed.

"Okay, we are ready to begin," Robbie said, as he took Grace's pocketbook from her shoulder.

Chapter 20 - The Betrayal

Over the next two weeks, Grace's bruises started to heal. Robbie showed up with roses and cards, and told her how sorry he was for everything, but now that they were engaged, she belonged to him, officially.

When Grace started talking about breaking off the engagement and their relationship, he started.

"Don't screw with me! I will ruin your life." And then continued, "You think what I did to *you* was bad, that's nothing. Have you forgotten that I have the keys to your mother's office?"

Grace looked at him, bewildered. So he continued. "Remember a few weeks ago, you wanted to know why I asked you to marry me? Well, I will tell you why, slut. I have the keys to your mother's office! Do you know what that means? I could wipe her out! I know where she keeps the company's checkbook! All I would have to do is have *you* forge her signature. You used to do it in high school, right? To go play with Dan? You will write her a note saying you're sorry, but you want to spend the rest of your life with me, and you needed some money to start fresh somewhere. And I'm . . . a rich man."

"And where does that leave me?" Grace asked, terribly scared now.

"Oh, you! I haven't thought about you, yet. I'm sure I could think of something!" He laughed madly and walked away.

* * *

Another Christmas came and went. Robbie didn't even show up this time. Grace sat with her family and hoped he had gotten hit by a car—maybe even killed. He called at nine o'clock to say that his sister was stuck at college in Providence, Rhode Island, and he had to pick her up. Grace was relieved.

"Robbie won't be coming over, everyone," she said with a smile in her voice. "Unfortunately, his sister is stuck at school and he's volunteered to go get her." Grace then picked up somebody's champagne glass and said, "Merry Christmas!"

The phone rang at six-thirty A.M. the next morning. Grace picked it up, thinking it was Robbie.

"Grace, is that you? I'm sorry to call so early, but is my Robert there?" Mrs. Gagnon sounded panic-stricken.

"Uh . . . no, Mrs. G. Robbie called last night to tell me he was picking Nancy up at school. He's not home, yet?" She was beginning to worry.

"Grace, Nancy came home two nights ago."

Grace thanked Mrs. Gagnon for calling and told her she would try one of his college friends. Maybe he lied and went to a party. As she reached for the phone, she remembered Shawn. *I bet he'll know where he went,* Grace thought. Shawn worked with Robbie in the security office. Shawn and Grace had become somewhat friends, until Robbie told her not to talk to him anymore.

"I don't want you being friends with my friends," he griped.

Grace had hardly ever talked to Shawn again, until today.

"Good morning, Shawn, and Merry Christmas. This is Grace Preston." Grace's palms were sweating and her stomach ached.

"Hey, how's it going, Grace? Haven't seen you in a long time," Shawn answered. He was cute. He looked a little like actor Patrick Swayze, except without the dimples.

"Yeah, it's been a while. Um . . . sorry to call you at work, but I need to ask you something." Grace hesitated, and then went on to tell him the story of Robbie's mother calling, and her being worried, etc.

"Grace, I thought you guys broke up a while ago. Why is she still calling you?" Shawn inquired.

"What do you mean, Shawn? Why would you think we broke up?" Grace's face began to flush. *No, this isn't what I think it is,* she thought.

Shawn realized that he couldn't make up a lie, and decided to tell Grace the truth. He always liked her better than he did Robbie anyway.

"Well, Grace, Robbie is probably over at Melissa's. They've been together for months! Jeez! You didn't know?" Shawn sounded confused.

"Shawn, we're engaged!" Grace started to cry. "I'm sorry . . . thank you . . ." Her voice trailed, as she hung up the phone.

"Oh my God!" she exploded. "He can't do this to me! He can't treat me like this . . . hurt me like this . . . and start up with somebody else!" Grace was furious. She had been scared for her life, for her mother's career . . . she had been beaten, raped, and now he was cheating on her, too!

Mrs. Preston heard the yelling and ran into Grace's room. "Honey, what is going on in here? Your room is a disaster area! What are you doing?"

Grace was in the process of tearing the memory album to shreds, page by page, and throwing them all over her room.

"Mom, Robbie slept over at some girl's house last night. Melissa. Her name is Melissa." Grace fell back onto the bed as she repeated her name.

"I told you he was no good!" Grace's mother was furious. "Oh . . . you better *not* go back to him after this. I hope you've realized what a jerk he is!"

She ranted and raved for several minutes about him, until she turned and noticed Grace was holding her stomach, and rocking back and forth, crying.

"Mom, how could he do this to me?"

Grace knew her mother wouldn't understand the question, because it was too complex. How could he do what? Beat her, rape her, force her to pay for her own diamond, cheat on her? Which did she mean? Even Grace didn't know.

* * *

The phone rang at seven A.M. It was Robbie.

"Babe . . . hi . . . I'm home," Robbie said weakly.

Grace was crying. "Robbie, who is she?"

"Who, Honey?" Robbie asked, innocently.

"Robbie, I'm not an idiot! I know you like to think I am, but I am far from it!" Grace was furious. "I want to know why you put me through all this for two damned years, and then you have the audacity to cheat on me, too?"

"Oh, I don't have time for this bullshit. I've got to call Melissa and let her know I got home okay. See ya!"

Robbie hung up the phone and Grace immediately dialed his number. She got a busy signal. *Oh, this is rich!* She fumed. Grace tried his number for twenty minutes. She was crying and screaming. She started running around the house kicking the walls and slamming doors. Her mother thought she had gone mad.

"Grace, what is wrong with you? Robert is not worth this! Stop torturing yourself!"

Grace's mother could not understand why she was acting crazy, and Grace couldn't even *begin* to tell her.

Chapter 21 - Robbie's plan

Melissa, I know! I didn't want her to find out either! Shit! What are we going to do?" Robbie asked as he ran his fingers furiously through his hair, and paced the floor of his bedroom.

"Well, Robert, you better think of something! What the hell was your mother doing calling her anyway?" Melissa yelled into the receiver.

Melissa Alexandra Strolka was a security guard where Robbie worked. They had met over a year ago when he started working the night shift. She had met Grace once before, but doubted if Grace would remember. Melissa had been in Robbie's office, rubbing his shoulders and kissing his neck, when Grace arrived with Chinese food. It was Grace's night off, and she thought she'd surprise him. Melissa saw her from the window and left through the Executive Offices and went down the back stairwell, which led to the West Lobby. Robbie would find her later.

Melissa was five-feet tall, had short blond hair and wore three earrings in her left ear. She worked out at the local YWCA on a weekly basis, and could probably bench over 150 pounds. She drank hard liquor and smoked Marlboro's. Melissa wasn't the lady that Grace's parents had brought her up to be.

Robbie and Melissa had flirted before, had gone out after work for drinks, but he had never stayed with her overnight. Until last night.

"Mel, the only thing I can do is make up with the bitch. I'll make up some lie, and tell her I'm sorry. She'll forgive me, believe me," he said with a laugh. "I've got her trained!"

"Well, you better figure it out because you promised me we were gonna take off somewhere and I want to get out of this shit-hole town. I hate living in Massachusetts!"

Melissa slammed down the phone. She knew she had Robbie right where she wanted him. If he didn't make up with Grace, he couldn't get the money. If he couldn't get the money, he couldn't take Mel away. She would tell somebody the entire twisted plot if he couldn't take her away. *Yes,* she thought, *he'll do what I say.*

The phone rang around ten-thirty A.M. It was Robbie.

"Grace, I'd like to come over and talk to you about this," he said. "We've been through so much, baby, and I want things between us to be right again."

"Robbie, do you have any idea what you've done to me? You've done so damn much, and I can't stop you!" Grace cried. "I don't want to see you ever again. You can come over to take your ring back, but that's it!"

For the first time, Grace hung up the phone on him. Robbie was angry, but he had to remain calm. He called a florist, and had three dozen red roses delivered that morning. Each dozen was in a crystal vase, and each had a red ribbon and card attached. The first card read, "Grace, I love you!" The second read: "I love you twice as much as before." And the third: "I love you three times as much as ever! Love Always, Robbie." When they arrived, Grace was blow-drying her hair. The doorbell rang, and an elderly gentleman stood, in uniform, in the cold morning air.

"Excuse me, does Grace Preston live here?" he asked.

"Yes, I'm Grace," she answered, as she opened the glass door a crack to see his van in the driveway. *Harry's Florist* was printed on the side of the van.

"In that case, little darlin', I have something for you." He tipped his hat and ran over toward the van. Opening the sliding door, he pulled out the roses, and handed the vases to her one by one.

"Oh my God! These are beautiful!" Grace said.

Her mother was folding the laundry in the first floor bathroom when she heard Grace. She quickly ran up the stairs to see thirty-six long-stemmed red roses laid out on the living room table.

Grace thanked the man, and closed the door.

"Mom, check these out! Robbie just wasted over two hundred and forty bucks!" she laughed. "He's got to be crazy to think this will work!"

Grace's mother smiled and hugged her tightly. "Oh Honey, I really hope you mean this. You won't go back to him, will you?"

"God, no! Not after this! Mom, you just don't understand what this has done to me. I feel like I've completely snapped," Grace said, as she walked into the kitchen.

Just then the doorbell rang. Grace ran down the stairs and opened the door. As she did, she looked at Robbie hard, and walked up the stairs. He followed.

"Mom, will you excuse us, please?" Grace asked, as her mother put away the morning breakfast dishes.

Without a word, Mrs. Preston walked past the two of them, shot Robbie a look, and went down the hall into her room. How she wished her husband had taken the day off.

Chapter 22 - The Apology

Grace sat nervously on a kitchen chair, while Robbie paced back and forth for a few minutes. He wore blue jeans and a blue and white striped polo shirt.

"Grace," he began, "I love you with all my heart, and I need you to know that. I am sorry about lying to you, but I had no choice. I stole some food from the lounge last week and one of the security guards saw me. She wanted to meet me the other night and talk about it. She said that if I didn't meet her, she would tell my boss that I stole the stuff, and I'd get fired." Robbie was beginning to sweat. He needed her to believe him.

"Robbie, who is Melissa? Is she the security guard that saw you?" Grace probed. "Why didn't you tell me, and why did Shawn say that you two have been together for months?" Grace asked.

Good, she believes me, he thought. "Well baby, first of all . . . who is Shawn?" Robbie asked, as he took a seat next to her at the kitchen table.

"When your mother called me to see if you were here, I thought about where you could possibly be. I figured I'd call your office. Shawn was working and I figured he might know because you guys work together all the time," Grace answered.

"Shawn doesn't know shit! I can't believe he told you that about Mel and me," Robbie yelled. "He's the one who's been after Mel for over six months and she won't even look at him. That's probably why he lied to you, Babe."

Grace sat for a few minutes and thought hard. "Well, Robbie, I don't know what to believe. Shawn has no reason to lie to *me*."

"Honey, listen to me. Melissa is just a guard that works for me. We talked things over last night and she's not going to say anything as long as I see about getting her a raise. That won't be a problem. I'm sorry I lied to you, but I was ashamed." As Robbie said this, he took her hand from across the table and started to cry.

"Robbie, you didn't even come home! And it was Christmas! Where'd you go?" Grace knew it was over. What could he say? She knew he was wrong. Their relationship would never be the same.

Robbie sat for a moment and thought about an answer. Obviously knew that she knew he was lying. "Grace, please! I'm sorry," he begged. "I didn't mean to ruin everything. This relationship means the world to me . . . please don't throw it away."

Grace withdrew her hand, slid off the one and a half karat diamond ring, and handed it to him. "Robbie," she said, "I don't think you and I will ever be the same. I feel differently now. It's like a part of me snapped and I'm back into reality. I don't want to spend the rest of my life like this." Finally, Grace had said it. She had broken up with him. It was over.

"Grace, you can't do this! I won't let you!" he spouted as he stood. "Nobody will ever have you. You're dirty."

Grace stood, closed her eyes and swallowed hard. "Robbie, please leave," she said, as she walked down the stairs into the foyer. She opened the solid oak door, and waited for him to follow.

Within moments, Robbie came down the stairs. He took Grace's hand as he walked to the door, careful for her mother not to hear him. He led her out to the front steps.

"Grace, maybe you didn't understand when I told you before, but I *will* kill you. And if you decide to go somewhere, I will find you. You cannot escape me . . . ever!" Robbie was now squeezing Grace's hand tightly. As she tried to push away from him, he suddenly let go, causing her to fall on the brick steps.

Robbie laughed. "I'll see you tomorrow, Honey," he said, as he blew her a kiss good-bye.

Chapter 23 - Grace's Plan

"Honey, what was *that* all about?" Grace's mother met her at the top of the stairs and took her arm. "I saw him grab your wrist. Are you okay?"

Grace gave her mother a hug and moved back into the kitchen. Sitting again on the beige woven kitchen chair, she started to cry.

"Oh, Mom. I can't take it anymore. I just want to go on with my life now. I'm so . . . tired." Grace was crying almost uncontrollably now. Her mother walked behind her and hugged her neck.

"Honey, it's okay. Everything is going to be okay now. You have your father and me. We love you very much, you know." Grace's mother began to cry, leaving a trail of brown mascara down her tanned face.

"I know, Mom. I really do. Thanks," Grace whispered, as she started to rise. "You know, I think I'd like to be alone for a while. I'll be in my room, okay?"

"Okay, I'll call you when dinner's ready."

Grace sat in her room and listened to Carly Simon's, *My Romance* CD all day. She tried to remember the good times, the times when Robbie wasn't hitting her, mocking her, raping her. She cursed him for taking her virginity in such a grotesque way. Looking at herself in the mirror, she asked, "Why?" She wanted to know how she had become so frightened of him over the past two years, and more importantly how a single human being could destroy everything she stood for, everything that *was* her. Four hours passed. Grace had been devising a plan of her own. For the first time in two years, she was actually thinking for herself. She put Robbie out of her head and concerned herself with *her* life.

"Honey, dinner's ready," Elizabeth yelled from the dining room, her voice echoing through the hall and into Grace's room. Yes, tonight they would eat in the dining room.

Elizabeth had spent the day preparing an Italian sauce for Grace's favorite dinner, chicken Parmesan. It had been her favorite since she was a little girl. Every birthday, Grace requested it for dinner, followed by a chocolate cake with chocolate frosting. Grace knew she was spoiled, but she truly appreciated it and her parents.

Grace walked slowly toward the kitchen, and noticed the light coming from the dining room. "Mom, you didn't have to do this." Grace beamed, as she took the empty seat located at the head of the table. The tablecloth was mauve lace. Her mother bought it for last Easter, but had used the white lace one instead. The cream-colored linen napkins were placed inside the brass napkin rings, and the gold silverware glistened under the chandelier. Her father sat at the other head seat, while Grace's mother sat beside him, on his right. Richard and his fiancée, Mary, sat on his left. Grace felt as if she would begin to cry, but instead she looked around the table and smiled.

"Thanks guys for being here. I had a bad day."

Grace laughed, for the first time in quite a while. She looked pale. Her skin was sallow and her big brown eyes were bloodshot. She was so tired. "Mom, Dad, and you guys too," Grace began, as she pointed to her brother and sister-in-law to be, "I have spent the past five or so hours in my room. I did a lot of thinking and I have a plan."

"A plan for what, Grace?" Richard asked as he raised a forkful of chicken to his mouth. He and Mary weren't as aware of the goings on in Grace's life as her mother and father were.

"I am going to move out . . . Now everyone, don't make faces—just hear me out for a minute," Grace said, as she saw the faces of the family drop. "If you all don't know by now, I broke up with Robbie today. I mean, gave back the ring and everything."

"Grace, what made you decide to do it now? Mom and Dad have been telling you for two years that he was no good," Richard said.

"I know, Richard, but I needed to realize some things on my own, and now that I did, I think the best thing for me to do is move someplace where he can't find me." Grace continued, "Now, I looked in the paper just a little while ago, and found some places that I think I could afford if I got one more job. Besides, I only have a year or so left in school, if I keep going during the summers." Grace stopped talking and waited for a response from her parents.

"Honey, are you sure this is what you want to do? I mean, you don't have to move out. Your father will go over and talk to his parents and tell him not to bother you anymore." Mrs. Preston sat confused. Why would her daughter want to move out of such a lovely home, to live alone somewhere?

"No, Mom . . . you can't talk to Robbie or his parents. You don't understand! Please! I need to do this without him knowing. I need to get away!"

Grace's voice started to rise, and her dinner was getting cold. She stabbed at the chicken, as she lowered her head. She wanted them to understand. "See, if I move out, I can concentrate all my efforts on school. I haven't been able to lately and I want to graduate with a good GPA. Plus, I'll be working another job so I'll be able to afford it. And Mom, can you take me off the schedule on those days when Robbie is working?"

"Well, as it is, the girls are taking your spot. Just let me know what days you can work and the time, and I'll redo the schedule. What else will you do for work?" Grace's mother was beginning to take her daughter seriously.

"I already called today for a counter girl position at a dry cleaner in Braintree. It'll be twenty hours a week. Of course, I have to go in and interview, but if I can't get a job as a counter girl, I should just give it up, huh?" Grace was laughing again.

They finished eating and moved into the living room where Grace explained to her mother and father how badly she needed to get away. When her father confronted her with the possibility that Robbie had hit her, she still denied it.

"No, Dad, I just want to move out so I can get myself back together. I mean, I've been with him for over two years now, and this is going to have to be a complete break up. I want to do this quickly so he won't know. If he comes here, you guys can just say that I moved out. I think it'll work."

Grace went on to explain that her schoolwork would be of utmost importance, and she could have some peace and quiet for a change. She told them how much she hated studying at his house all the time and she couldn't wait until she had a place of her own.

"Well, Honey," Grace's father began, "your mother and I are behind you one-hundred percent. If you want us to go looking at places with you, we will . . . just don't go too far away."

"Oh, I love you guys!" Grace started to cry and hugged her parents. Maybe, just maybe, she could finally begin the process of healing.

Chapter 24 - 1990

The following morning, Grace and her parents decided to take a day off from work and go apartment hunting. They wanted to find her the best possible place to live, at the best possible price.

When Robbie arrived at her house at 11:30 A.M., there was nobody home. He rang the doorbell and looked through the windows to see if she might have been there, but after twenty minutes, he left. He would come back later.

Grace and her parents found an apartment ad in Quincy, near her father's old house, and called the landlord. They got an appointment for 12:30 P.M.

"Oh, I hope this place is nice. It says here that it's only five hundred and twenty-five dollars a month, and that includes heat and hot water. That's pretty good, huh?" Grace said from the back seat of the car, as her father drove up the hill and into the driveway. The small red brick apartment building had a well-kept front lawn; it was off the main road, and seemed relatively quiet.

Grace's father got out of the red 1987 Chrysler LeBaron and walked over to help his wife and daughter out of the car. Then they walked down the steep hill toward the front entrance.

As he reached for the metal door handle, a man wearing faded jeans, a plaid shirt, and bifocals opened the door. He was an older gentleman, in his early sixties most likely, and his gray hair was tousled. He smiled as he led the three inside.

"Welcome. You must be the Preston's. Nice to meet you," he said with a grin. "My name is Henry Wortheim." His hands were stained with white paint, and he reeked of turpentine. As Mr. Preston shook his hand, Henry noticed the paint and said, "Oh, excuse me . . . painting the vacant one-bedroom." He chuckled and wiped his hands back and forth on his jeans.

He led them to the third floor and stopped before apartment number eleven. "Well, this is it. Excuse the mess, but I'm renovating." The door was ajar, and Grace peeked inside. "I've put in a new carpet, as you can see—beige and brown. Pretty common color. People seem to like the neutrals, you know." Henry led them inside. "It's a pretty good size. You've got a full kitchen, living room and over there is your bathroom with full bath."

As the Preston family wandered through the apartment, Henry continued, "Here's the bedroom. Pretty good size, I think, with the two windows. Gets pretty sunny in this apartment. Over there is your walk-in closet. Women just love that!" He laughed as he opened the double doors.

"Wow!" was all Grace could express. The place was fabulous. The kitchen had plenty of cabinet space; the living room was huge and very sunny. She loved it. She started thinking of all the things she could buy, the pots and pans, the plants, the coffee table . . .

"Could we have a moment to discuss this?" Mrs. Preston asked, as Henry started to clean the woodwork.

"Oh sure. I'll just wait outside. If you decide you want it, I'll give you an application and we . . . well, I'll let you discuss it," Henry said, as he pushed the loose piece of hair out of his eyes and walked out into the hall.

Once Henry was outside, Grace said, "Mom, Dad . . . I want this place. It's so perfect for me, and only a few minutes to the highway. I'll be to school in no time at all." She beamed, as she stood in the middle of the living room and threw her hands into the air. "I can finally be free!" she exclaimed.

Her mother and father looked at each other and walked toward Grace. Mr. Preston hugged his daughter. "Mr. Wortheim, we're ready for you now," he said.

As Henry entered the apartment again, he held the application in his hand. "I was hoping the answer would be *yes*. It's good to see a mother and father shopping for an apartment. I like you both and I wish there were more parents like you in this world," he said, as he smiled at Grace. "Well, little lady, it looks like you've got yourself an apartment."

"Don't you have to do a credit check on me?" Grace asked almost nervously, because she hadn't paid a dime toward the engagement ring, and the credit card had been sent to a collection agency.

"No, no. Your parents came with you. That shows me a lot. I'm supposed to take first, last and a security, but I'll just take first for now. When you move your stuff, I'll take last. You don't have to pay the security. I hope my wife doesn't kill me." He laughed, as he wandered down the hall, down the two flights of stairs, and back into the lobby.

Grace turned to her parents as they started down the steps. "I can't thank you enough for coming with me today."

"Well, this is a secure place, and I like Henry. He lives only four miles away, so if you need anything fixed, he'll be right over," Mrs. Preston said while eyeing the pale blue paint in the hall. "Is he going to repaint these walls, or are they going to stay blue?" she asked. Her colors were peach and beige. She didn't care much for blue.

"Oh, I don't care. I couldn't get over the apartment itself, it was beautiful," Grace said. She moved down the stairs onto the second floor landing, where a window displayed the back parking lot. There were trees to the left and right of the cemented lot, and directly behind it stood a white house with an enclosed porch. A swing set could be seen from above the fence. She just knew she would love it here.

Mr. Preston followed behind the two ladies, and thanked Henry again for showing them the apartment. "Henry, it was a pleasure to meet you," he said, as he shook his hand. He then pulled on the heavy glass entrance door, and showed his family to the car. Mr. Wortheim waved from the front lawn as they drove away.

* * *

Upon returning home, Grace saw the blue Mazda Protege' in the driveway. She flinched. Robbie was waiting for her, and she realized this would not be an easy road. Her father pulled in the garage and opened the door for his wife and daughter. The three stood together as Robbie got out of his car and walked closer to them.

"Hi, Mr. P., Mrs. P.," he said softly. "I know you probably don't want me here, but I really would like to talk to Grace, if that's okay with you."

Robbie's eyes were red and he hadn't shaved. He had spent the night with Melissa, at her apartment in Boston, and she told him not to shave.

"It looks better if you don't shave . . . like you've been out all night thinking of her or something," Melissa had explained. "She's stupid enough to buy that!" Mel laughed, as she stepped out of the shower and wrapped a white towel around her body. Robbie was looking at himself in the bathroom vanity mirror. He had already put the shaving cream on his face.

"So, you think it'll look better if I don't shave?" he asked, as he began washing off the Gillette foam.

"Yeah, and when you get dressed, splash some liquor on you. She knows you hardly ever drink, and if you do that, she'll think you really miss her . . . I can't believe your mother fucked up like this. She ruined everything." Melissa picked up the red lighter and lit a Marlboro.

After Robbie was dressed, he did what Mel said, and headed to Grace's house. She wasn't there, so he had to come back later.

"So, can I talk to you, Grace?" Robbie begged now. He turned to her father and started crying. "Mr. Preston, I know you don't want me near your daughter, but I really love her. I want her back. I want to marry her." Robbie leaned against the LeBaron with his back to Grace and her mother. Both of them were shocked.

"Robert, I don't know what's been going on between you and my daughter, but I do know that the engagement is off. If Grace doesn't want to talk to you that is her decision, not mine," Mr. Preston said, as he walked away.

Grace walked behind her father and into the house, and Mrs. Preston followed. Grace shut the door and started up the stairs. Suddenly, she heard Robbie's horn beeping. It started with a few short taps and within a minute became one long screaming sound. She opened the door. He stopped. "Robert, knock if off!" she hollered.

"Grace, please . . . I love you! Don't leave me!" Robbie was wiping his eyes with the sleeve of his bomber jacket. He opened the car door and stepped onto the pavement. Grace watched from inside the house.

"Grace . . . I . . . open the door," he said, walking closer to the front steps. "I want us to be together." He had reached the top step. Grace was watching from behind the glass door. She locked it while he started over, and she felt safe.

"Robbie, go away. And don't beep the horn like that again, or I'll call the cops."

Grace's eyes began to fill and a tear escaped, falling onto the beige carpet below, without making a sound. "Please, don't make me do that. I just want you to go away. It's over."

Then she slammed the door and walked downstairs, where her mother and father waited, patiently. Grace heard the car engine start and she peered out the window. Robbie was driving away.

Grace sat on the brown leather sofa, and started crying. "I'm not strong enough for this. What if he does this every day? I just can't take it."

"Honey, let me call Mr. Wortheim. I'll see if we can get you moved in sooner than a month. It looked like he was almost finished renovating, so maybe you can pay him a little extra and move in sooner."

Mr. Preston sat beside Grace while Mrs. Preston looked out the window, making sure that Robbie was really gone. She walked over to Grace, kissed the top of her head, and went upstairs. She was becoming frightened.

Chapter 25 - Mom's Office

"Elizabeth, I know you took a few days off, but I think you need to get in here . . . as soon as you can." It was Jesse from the office. She had worked for Elizabeth as her secretary for over five years. Jesse was in her late twenties. She didn't care much for makeup, unless she was going on the show floor to deal directly with exhibitors. Most of the time, she wore pants and heavy sweaters—even during the summer season, because of the air-conditioned office, she said. She was heavyset, but well groomed. Her personality lacked tact however, and Elizabeth had reprimanded her on more than one occasion for her lack of politeness toward customers on the phone.

Elizabeth was in the process of making scrambled eggs, bacon and toast for her and Grace. Richard had left for work already. Elizabeth was wearing her puppy slippers that Grace had bought her for Christmas two years ago. They were brown and had the face of a puppy on each foot. She loved these slippers. Her nightgown was peach flannel—another gift from Grace on Mother's Day. As she listened to Jesse, her heart pounded. She put the spatula down next to the stove and walked with the phone into the living room.

"Jesse, just calm down and speak slowly. Now what happened?" Elizabeth asked, one hand holding the phone while she nervously twisted her frosted locks. She sat on the first step leading down toward the foyer, and listened.

"Well, I came in this morning at eight-thirty, as usual. When I went up the stairs and down the hall, I noticed your office was open—a little. And I know you lock it every night. Then I remembered you were out yesterday. Now I know the door was locked yesterday because I remember needing something in there, but decided to wait until you came in." Jesse had a habit of rambling and couldn't seem to get a grip in an emergency.

"Jesse, please . . . just get to the point. What happened?" Elizabeth was becoming impatient and a little nervous herself.

"Okay. When I saw that your door had been opened, I walked in. The computers had been turned on and your desk was unlocked. I went over to your computer and a message appeared . . . well, to make a long story short, your billing for the past three months has been deleted. Customers, amounts of deposits and balances . . . everything!" Jesse stopped talking and waited. Elizabeth gasped, and then was unable to speak for a few moments. "Liz . . . you still there?" Jesse asked.

"I'll be right there!" Elizabeth said curtly. She walked back into the kitchen in a daze, unwrapped herself from the long phone cord and hung up the phone. "Grace!" she called to her daughter, who was still in her bedroom, probably listening to the stereo.

"Yeah, what's up, Mom?" Grace came into the kitchen, wearing a gray college sweatshirt and flannel shorts. Her hair was pulled up in a ponytail. "Breakfast ready?" she asked, and then noticed her mother's face. "What happened, Mom?"

"I need you to be honest with me, Honey. Does Robbie have access to my office?" Mrs. Preston was running her hands through her hair and pacing.

"Why? What's going on?" Grace saw the terrified look in her mother's eyes, and became frightened herself. *I will wipe her out*, she suddenly heard in the back of her mind. Robbie had said that he would do it, but of course, he had just been bluffing—hadn't he?

"Please, just answer me, Grace. Does he or doesn't he have access to my office? And when I say office, I mean my computers, desk, everything!"

"Yeah, I think he does. I mean, he has the keys to *everybody's* office. He's security. As far as the computers go, he definitely knows how to manipulate them. He's going to be a hardware engineer when he graduates . . . or is it a software engineer? I don't know."

"Grace, somebody has been in my office, and they wiped out the past quarter's billing information. Jesse says it's gone! *Everything!* All the tenants who owe payments for this month, all the tenants' balances, addresses . . . everything!"

Elizabeth walked back and forth, through the kitchen and into the hallway. She started for her bedroom. She had to get dressed. *If Robbie was the one who did this, there'll be hell to pay!* she thought.

Moments later, Elizabeth appeared in a red wool skirt and white blouse. She grabbed her brown mink coat from the hall closet and threw it around her shoulders. In an instant, she was gone.

Grace sat on the steps in bewilderment. Would Robbie have really done that to her mother? He had made threats before, but would he really risk his job over it? How could he get away with it? Grace called her mother on the car phone and explained verbally what she had just thought. "Mom, I don't think he would jeopardize his job just to get even with me. Maybe the system just crashed," Grace suggested.

"Grace, you know I never liked Robbie. I don't trust him—never have. Have your father call that Henry character and see if you can move in right away. I don't want Robert anywhere near you."

Elizabeth sped into the exposition center. She parked her Lincoln in front of the entrance doors and ran inside. When she reached her main office door, Jesse was waiting for her. She too, was pacing.

"Elizabeth, I called Mark Page . . . you know, the systems guy for the computers if they go down or something like that. He's on his way in."

Jesse opened Elizabeth's office door and showed Elizabeth the computer. The screen was flashing "Deleted" and the keyboard appeared to be locked up. Hitting the *Escape* key or any other key seemed to have no effect.

Elizabeth walked over to her mahogany desk and sat in her chair. Opening the top drawer, where she usually kept the employees' payroll information and company checkbook, she found things disheveled. Papers were scattered on the floor. About one week prior, she had transferred all the payroll information, the company checkbook, and various other items to a metal file cabinet. Jesse had ordered those months ago, and they had just arrived. Elizabeth wanted to reorganize her office, and Jesse had been eager to help. All employee information was alphabetized and put in individual hanging folders in the bottom cabinet. The middle cabinet drawer held tenant information, backlogs of checks paid to Elizabeth's company, etc. The top metal cabinet drawer was for the company checkbook and miscellaneous billing items. It was secured with a lock and key. The key, Elizabeth had put on her personal key chain.

Elizabeth dialed the security office and asked for Robbie's boss, George. George Hinkman was a pleasant man in his late thirties. He was married and had two children. Elizabeth and George had worked together for many years, and were friends. "George, I wanted to let you know that my office has been tampered with, and whoever was here erased my past quarter's billing information." Elizabeth continued, before giving him a chance to speak. "Now George, whether you knew this or not, Grace broke off her engagement and I think Robbie—well, I hate to put the blame on someone until I know for sure—but I wouldn't put it past him to do something like this and—"

George interrupted. "Elizabeth, you are making quite an accusation. Robbie wasn't on duty last night. He called in sick. The only person I could get was Melissa Strolka.

Are you familiar with her? You can talk to her if you like. She'll be in about three."

"Okay, thanks George. I'll let you know."

Mark Page, the computer guy, arrived at one-thirty in the afternoon. He was carrying a black leather briefcase and a larger box, which Elizabeth assumed was filled with tools. Mark was rather thin, with red hair and blue eyes. He looked a little like Richard Cunningham from "Happy Days," a television show that came out in the 1970's. He worked hard and rarely spoke to anyone, so nobody knew anything about his personal life.

"Well," he said, after examining the computer for a few minutes, "I was able to retrieve your billing information. It's a little technical, but basically, I went to the hard drive and recovered the file. I think whoever did this just wanted to scare you. Do you know anyone who might have access to your computer?"

"Yes I do, Mark. I can't thank you enough for reestablishing these accounts." Elizabeth's face finally relaxed a little and she realized how tense she had been all day. "I'll have the locks in my office changed today," she said to him as Mark got out of the maroon leather chair and stood near her office door. She shook his hand, made promises of a luncheon soon, and he waved good-bye.

When Elizabeth returned home, she talked to her husband and Grace about the entire situation. She knew that Robbie was the one who had almost destroyed her computer system. She remembered hearing the name, Melissa, before and realized on her way home that Grace had mentioned her in connection with Robbie. *Of course! He calls in sick to work, Melissa takes over. Robbie shows up after everyone leaves and she lets him in.* It was all becoming clear to her as she pulled into the driveway. "I just can't prove it, damn it!" she yelled, as Grace and her father looked at each other, startled. They saw such hate in Elizabeth's eyes when she talked about Robbie.

"Honey, all we can do is change the locks to your office, for now," Jack said. "You talked to George, so he is at least aware of it. If Robbie tries something else, they'll fire him. That's all." Jack Preston always remained calm in the worst possible situations. He was their safe harbor. "Now, I'll run down to the hardware store, and install the locks myself. In the meantime, Grace, you start packing. I talked to Henry and he said you can move in next week."

Grace's face lit up as she squealed and hugged her mother and father. "Oh! Thank God! Daddy, thank you so much!"

Grace ran into her room and started going through her belongings, trying to decide where to start.

Chapter 26 - Grace Moves Out

It didn't take Grace long to pack. She didn't have many real belongings—just her bedroom set and desk. Of course, her clothes took three trips back and forth to the apartment, but she didn't mind. Her family helped her move, since she had lost all the friends she had over the past two and a half years. After she was established and back on her feet again, she would try to contact those friends.

Afraid that Robbie would follow her and discover where she was moving to, she rented a car to move her belongings. Robbie still had *their* car, and until she could afford to buy another, she needed to take precautionary measures. She moved only on days that he worked until 11:00P.M.

Grace was still extremely frightened. Although she knew she was doing the right thing, still she was apprehensive. Over the past weekend and on into the beginning of the week, Robbie had called every night. If Grace answered, she would hang up, and if her parents answered, they would say she was in the shower or at the store. It was hard for them to maintain their composure when he would call, because both of them wanted to call the police and get him arrested for tampering with Elizabeth's files. Unfortunately, they couldn't prove it, and if they said anything, Robbie would probably harass them and their daughter even more.

* * *

Robbie knew exactly what Grace was doing. He knew she was moving to Quincy, because he had Melissa following her. He had showed her once before where Grace lived, and on Melissa's nights off, she watched and waited. Grace didn't know it, but her moving out was one of the worst mistakes of her life. She thought it was a chance to start over, to get herself and her life back on track. But Robbie saw it as an opportunity to get her alone, where she couldn't go running home to Daddy. She was playing right into his trap. When he had told her on the steps that day ". . . no matter where you go, I'll find you . . ." he knew it would get her thinking about running away or moving somewhere. He knew her like the back of his hand, and decided that he would wait until he devised another plan. After the fiasco with her mother's office, he wanted to lay low for a while. He wouldn't be able to do much from a jail cell, so he would bide his time.

Within two weeks, Grace was settled into her new *home*. Her father had a lot of friends in the automobile industry, and he was able to pick up a good used car for a little under a thousand dollars. She could pay them back when she graduated, he told Grace. Her mother took her for her first official food shop, at the local supermarket, and the total came to well over $125.00! Her mother took care of it and Grace carried the bundles up the stairs and into her kitchen. Grace hoped it wouldn't cost that much ever again.

Slowly, she decorated the apartment with floor plants, wall hangings, and she hung potholders and coffee mugs in her kitchen. It was starting to look *homey*. Her bedroom furniture was a light oak, and the curtains were peach satin with lace trim. She quickly filled the walk-in closet and neatly arranged all of her winter sweaters, suits, skirts and jeans that she wore to school. She couldn't have picked a better time to move out. School didn't start for another two and a half weeks, and she could concentrate on decorating her place.

The bathroom was large enough to put in another wall cabinet. Her father made it for her and she placed all her shampoos, conditioners and moisturizers inside. She put up a peach shower curtain with matching peach and beige towels and floor mats. Grace loved it here.

The curtains in the living room were beige and they draped nicely to the floor. In front of the window overlooking the quiet street, she put a beige tweed couch that she bought at Jordan's Warehouse. She got it on sale for only $350.00. The left and right sides of the couch pulled out and turned into recliners. She wouldn't have been able to afford it had her parents not paid for the first month's rent. They wanted to help her out and let her know they were proud of her.

When Grace bought the sofa, she spotted an oak coffee table beside it. She told her parents about it and asked them if they liked it. Two days later, Grace came home from work, went up the stairs into her apartment and found it there, with a huge peach ribbon around it, and a note: "We love you! Mom and Dad." Grace gave her parents an extra set of keys in the event she ever misplaced hers. She couldn't believe how great this was.

Grace's first day back at school was nerve racking. She was afraid she would turn a corner and see Robbie, or find him waiting in the parking lot. She had a different car, and she would reschedule the times of some of her classes for when she knew Robbie would be working.

Grace also had to figure out when to fit in her jobs. After spending the better half of the day in the Administration Office, she had scheduled five courses. She would go to school on Tuesdays and Thursdays from 8:30 A.M. to 7:00 P.M. She would work Monday, Wednesday and Friday from 10:00A.M. to 3:00 P.M. at the insurance company. Tuesday and Thursday nights from 8:00 to 11:00 at the exposition center (because Robbie's schedule had changed to Monday, Wednesday and Friday). On Monday, Wednesday and Friday she would work from 4:00 to 7:00 P.M., as well as on Sunday mornings, at the dry cleaners. *Whew!* she thought, as she wrote furiously in her daytime planner, *I hope I can handle all this!*

Driving home from school, Grace's mind raced. She couldn't wait to tell her family how she had gotten all the classes she wanted, and at the times she wanted, and to show them her new work schedule. She could survive after all. A few times over the past month, she had thought of Robbie. She remembered the time she called in sick to work and he showed up at her second story bedroom window at 11:30 P.M. with a basket full of homemade chocolate chip cookies. On a napkin he had written, "Count how many chips there are in each cookie and total them up. When you do, multiply it by 100 and that is how much I love you."

She laughed for a moment as she remembered her father's expression as he saw two long legs pass the first floor window. He had been watching television and his wife was sleeping. He thought it was a burglar and ran up the stairs, heart pounding. When he reached the top step, he heard laughter coming from Grace's window. He knocked and then immediately entered, to find Robbie hanging onto the window.

"Oh, hi Mr. P. Hope I didn't scare ya, but I wanted to give Grace these cookies I made. I was going to leave them in her car, but she locked it. Of all the times, she has to lock it tonight." Robbie laughed as he told the story about sneaking into the lounge kitchen and making the cookies.

Mr. Preston laughed too, said goodnight and shut her door. He had been young once, and sometimes still acted that way toward his wife.

Grace pulled into her driveway, gathered up her planner and newly bought books, and started for the front door. She was fumbling in her purse for the key to her apartment. She looked up and her heart stopped. He was standing at the front door with a bouquet of roses in his hand.

"Hello Grace," he chirped. "I've missed you." Robbie was dressed in his security uniform of blue and gray, and as Grace dropped her books she started to scream. Robbie quickly released the roses and grabbed Grace's face, cupping his hands around her mouth. She bit hard, but he didn't flinch. "C'mon, I want to see your new place."

Grace was terrified. *How could he know where she lived? She'd been so careful.* "Robbie, let go!" she mumbled, as he released his grip. "How did you . . . where did you come from?" she asked, tears forming in her big brown eyes. He had been right. *She would never escape him.*

"Grace, you didn't listen to me. I told you when you broke off our engagement that I would find you. I knew you'd think about moving out, getting your life back together, blah, blah, blah. You're so predictable." He laughed, while taking the key from her hand. "Now, you're going to talk to me and that's the end of it." Robbie opened the door and watched her as she led him to apartment number eleven. *Damn him!*

Turning the key and opening the door, Robbie seemed surprised. "Grace, this place looks great. I must admit, you do have a certain knack with that domestic stuff. My mother always said you'd make a great wife." Robbie waltzed over toward the kitchen area, and spotted the hanging potholders and mugs. "Nice touch. Adds a bit of home to the place, huh?"

"Robbie, please tell me what you want—and then leave. I mean, it's over between us. I've started to get myself back these past two months, and I'm starting to like me again. My parents and I are getting along a lot better and I haven't had to cover any bruises in over two months!" Grace began to cry. "Robbie . . . please just go away. Move on to somebody else and let me be."

"Grace, I didn't come over here to argue with you. I bought roses for Christ's sake! I want forgiveness and us to be engaged again. I really do." Robbie had taken off his blue jacket and seated himself on the sofa. He sat with his elbows resting on his knees, his hands folded between his legs, as if waiting to be reprimanded by angry parents.

"Robbie, please don't start this again. I know we had good times, but the bad far outweighed them. I wish it could be different, but you have a major problem. You are really abusive, and you don't even drink! That is so scary. What would happen if you did drink?" This was the first time the two had communicated in ages. Whenever Grace had started talking about his abuse in the past, he would deny it, swear at her, or walk away. This was different. He was actually listening.

"Grace, all I know is that I love you. Maybe that's why I get weird sometimes, and I hit you. But if you didn't make me jealous all the time, I wouldn't get mad." Robbie was still seated on the sofa. Grace was standing by the kitchen set.

"Robbie, I used to tell you all the time how much I loved you, but you didn't believe me. You started cursing and hitting me, and well . . . you know the rest. I don't want to spend the rest of my life with you like that. If you would agree to go to counseling or something like that, maybe it could work, but for now I've got to rebuild my self-esteem, and learn how to become *normal* again." Grace was finished. She sat in the kitchen chair of light unfinished wood, and waited. She was amazed that he hadn't hit her by now.

"Grace," he said, as he stood up and began to rummage through his pants pockets. "I want you to take this back. Don't answer me right now, and you don't even have to wear it, but if you ever decide you do want to wear it again, call me."

Robbie proceeded to take out a small box and handed it to Grace. As she opened it, she saw the engagement ring he had given her before. *What is going on?* she wondered. *What has happened to him?* Grace took the ring and held it for a few moments, then placed it back inside the box. She remembered when he had given it to her, and she began, once again, to become teary eyed.

"Well, that's all I wanted to say. Good-bye, Grace. I love you." Robbie walked over to her and kissed her gently on the mouth. It was like their first kiss in his office, almost three years ago. He smiled at her and opened the door, closing it behind him.

A few minutes after he left, the phone rang. It was Grace's mother. "So, how'd school go today? Did you get all the classes you wanted?"

Grace didn't know whether to tell her mother about Robbie. She had just begun to grow close to her again and she didn't want to lose that, but if she didn't, her mother was more than likely to find out. "Mom, Robbie was just here," she started.

"What are you talking about? Is this what your real plan was? To move out so that he could come over any time he pleased?" Grace's mother was furious. Jack heard her yelling and raced into the kitchen, where he saw his wife sitting at the table with the phone in her hand.

"No, Mom, I just came home a little while ago and Robbie was standing out front. He said he wanted to talk, and as it turns out, he gave me back my ring and asked me to think about us getting back together."

"Well, I certainly hope you're not going to consider it! You'd have to be out of your mind!" Grace's mother had stood and was pacing the kitchen floor. Jack was listening and pointing to the phone, mouthing, 'Grace?' She nodded and brushed him away. He went back downstairs to watch T.V. He would find out what was going on later.

"No, Mom. I'm not going back to him. I moved out so I could get away from him, remember?" Grace was hurt. She wanted to talk to her mother about this, not argue. She was exhausted. It had been a long day.

"Honey, I'm sorry for getting upset with you. It's just that you and your father and I are becoming a family again, like we used to be. I've missed you. I've missed the talks we used to have. When you started dating Robert, you became a different person, and now that you're becoming your old self again, I don't want to see you get consumed with him, anymore. We love you, Honey." Mrs. Preston's voice was shaky and she was becoming emotional. She was afraid for her daughter's life and now, finding out that he was back . . . it just terrified her.

Chapter 27 - Stalking Grace

The dry-cleaning store where Grace worked was less than ten minutes from Robbie's house. It was a small shop with five teenage girls who worked as counter help, two Portuguese men who worked in the back room, pressing shirts, and one Italian man, who cleaned the clothes.

Grace liked working with her new co-workers. The girls would come in to work with stories of the boys they liked, or the classes they skipped, and Grace hoped for just a moment that she could go back to those simpler days, before Robbie.

"So Grace, really, do you have a boyfriend?" Katie asked, as she tagged the white long sleeved cotton shirt to be starched. Katie was seventeen. She had long blond hair and sea green eyes. Her mother wanted her to go to modeling school in New York, but Katie's boyfriend, Rich, argued against it. Katie decided to stay in town, finish high school, and work part-time as a counter girl, instead.

Grace liked Katie. It was Katie who had trained her, just a few weeks ago, and they had shared dinner breaks. Katie had asked Grace just a few times before about a boyfriend. Grace brushed it off by saying that she was too busy with college and her jobs. "Too busy to even *study*!" she laughed, as the two sat on the redwood picnic table behind the store one night. Grace and Katie were becoming friends. Katie was the first person since Robbie that Grace had actually talked to, but she still kept a watchful eye on her surroundings. She was still scared.

"Nope. No boyfriend," Grace responded, as she placed the "Closed" sign on the glass door by the front of the store. It was a little past seven o'clock and she was tired. It had been a long day, but Grace knew it was worth it.

"Katie, I'll close up, you go on home. I'm sure Rick is waiting, right?" Grace said, as she winked at Katie.

"Oh, are you sure you don't mind?" Katie asked, while grabbing for her off-white leather pocketbook.

"No, I'm just gonna go home and crash anyway. I can't study tonight, I'm too tired," Grace replied. She still had about half an hour left before she could leave. The cash registers needed to be totaled and the money needed to be counted and put into the safe. The cleaning people would be in by eight o'clock, and she'd be done by then.

"Thanks Grace. You're the best," Katie said, as she waltzed out the back door and into the parking lot.

Grace waved through the front window as she watched Katie drive away. She caught a glimpse of the orange glow of the sun setting behind the liquor store across the street. A young couple, holding hands and eating ice cream cones, passed by Grace, and she smiled at them through the glass window.

It was just a few minutes past seven-thirty. Grace was locking the door behind her when she felt a hand across her mouth. Before turning around, she knew it was *him*. "Don't say a word!" he said, as he pressed his hand against her lips harder. "I just want to talk to you, that's all."

Grace's mind raced. Her heart began to pound, and the old familiar feeling of fear quickly returned. "Robbie, what do you want from me?" she pleaded. She was facing him now, and noticed that his face was unshaven and his eyes were bloodshot. It reminded her of the time in her driveway, not so long ago. He was wearing gray sweat shorts and a pale blue Ocean Pacific short sleeved shirt. The white Reebok sneakers she had given him for his last birthday were now dirty and worn.

"Grace, I want to talk to you," he repeated, as he grabbed her arm and led her to his car. Grace was pulling away and her brown leather flats were leaving marks on the soft dirt surface, as she dug her heel into the earth.

"Grace, don't screw with me! Get in the car!" Robbie opened the passenger door and kicked her leg. She tripped and fell against the window. "Get in the car!" Robbie pushed her until she fell into the seat. He quickly shut the door and locked it.

Grace was furious. As she started to grab for the handle to unlock the passenger door, he was already in the car and slapping her hand away. "What the hell is wrong with you?" Grace exclaimed as she looked wildly at Robbie, who was now holding both hands so that Grace wouldn't get out of the car.

She had spent the past few weeks praying that Robbie would leave her alone. Now that she was becoming herself again, she was also becoming a little stronger. She was regaining the closeness with her family and starting a friendship with Katie.

"Did you forget who you're talking to?" Robbie shouted as he reached up from her lap, releasing one of her hands from his grip, and slapped her mouth.

Grace opened the mirror on the sun visor, and noticed the blood on her bottom lip. She wasn't crying and was staring at herself in the mirror, with disgust in her eyes. Grace was tired of fixing bruises and fat lips. She was tired of dyeing her hair to suit *his* whims. As she reached in her purse for a tissue to blot her mouth, she felt the car vibrating. They were moving.

Grace's stomach was in knots again. "Robbie, where are we going?" Grace asked, frightened of his response.

He didn't answer, but laughed in an almost psychotic manner, and smiled as he patted her on the head. Grace wanted to open the door and just jump out, but Robbie was driving too fast.

Ten minutes later, they reached their destination. Robbie had taken her behind an old abandoned office building, which stood tall on the top of a steep hill and overlooked Scituate. She and Robbie had been there before, one New Year's Eve, years ago. He had picked her up at seven-thirty, dressed in a dark blue suit, and took her there.

When they pulled in behind the building, on top of the hill, she noticed a red blanket with tall white candles glowing briefly in the dark red wine, and a picnic basket of crackers, cheese and fresh strawberries. It was their first New Year's Eve together, and he wanted it to be special for her. Tonight, he brought her here for very different reasons.

"Grace, remember, when we first came here?" Robbie turned the ignition off and stared numbly through the front windshield, thinking about that night long ago. His voice had become softer, less threatening. "We came here on New Year's Eve," he said, while reaching for Grace's hands.

"Robbie, I remember," Grace said in a whisper. After a moment of silence, Grace became restless. "Please, can we just go? I don't want to be here," she said, while staring at the dirt left on the blue floormat from her shoes.

"You loved me then, Grace. We were inseparable. And now, you're afraid of me. I love you so much! Where did we go wrong?" Robbie asked as his voice started to shake. A tear fell from his eyes, and he quickly brushed it away. "Why don't you love me anymore?" he asked.

Oh, I don't believe this! Grace thought. It was now eight-forty and she was drained. She wanted to crawl into bed and stay there for weeks. "Robbie, we've *been* through this already. Yeah, maybe things were okay way back then, and from time to time, but honestly, this is ridiculous. I just want to go on with my life. I need to do this . . . without you." Grace spoke in an emotionless, monotone voice. She was still frightened of him, and her self-esteem was far from strong, but she was trying. Her lip stung as she licked her lips before continuing.

"I need to start over, to put this behind me and move on. Please let me." Grace had withdrawn her hand from him, and leaned toward him to start the car. He grabbed her hand.

"I don't want to go," Robbie hollered as he ripped the keys from the ignition and threw them into the back seat. "I don't want you to *move on*, either! You and I have a history together, damn it! You *belong* to me!" As Robbie's voice began to rise, Grace's face became pale. Before she could move, he pulled her into him as he tried to kiss her.

"Robbie, stop it! I want to go!" she yelled, as she jerked herself back into the passenger side door. She felt beads of perspiration forming on her forehead and contemplated whether it was because she was hot or just plain scared.

"Grace, you can't leave me! I gave you a ring, for Christ sakes! I own you!" Robbie was growing wild again. He yanked Grace's seat back with his left hand, while pressing his upper body on her chest, forcing her to lie back into the seat. "C'mon, baby, show me how much you love me," he whispered into her ear.

"Robbie, please, please don't hurt me!" Grace started to cry, as he lifted her pale yellow skirt, and pulled down her panties. He started to push himself against her and she felt a sharp pain in her lower abdomen. Her gynecologist had informed her months before that she had internal scarring and the possibility of her having children was slim. She remembered suddenly her doctor's inquiries and concerns. She wished she wouldn't have to go through this tonight. Her doctor would surely question her again.

When Robbie was finished, he reached for the handle of the passenger side window and unrolled it. He then unlocked the door with his left hand, and pushed it open. Robbie lifted himself off Grace, stepped onto the pavement, and started to walk toward the shrubs about ten feet away. Suddenly, Grace realized the keys were in the back seat. She quickly shut and locked the doors. She grabbed for the keys while sliding into the driver's seat. *I'll run him over!* she thought. Her stomach was churning. She had to do this right now. But before she could even turn the ignition, Robbie was reaching through the passenger window.

Grace started the car, as he struggled to get in. "What are you doing!" Robbie yelled, as he unlocked the passenger door and jumped in.

"Robbie, I'll kill you! Leave me alone!" Grace screamed, as she slapped his hand away from the ignition. "I will kill you!" Grace's expression was that of a mad woman. She was hitting his arm and slapping his body uncontrollably. When she scratched him in the eye, he started to bleed.

"You dumb shit!" Robbie yelled, as he grabbed at the keys once more and turned off the ignition. "You're a worthless piece of shit!" he said with disgust. "Get out of the car!"

"No!" Grace was defiant. She was finished with his control and obsessiveness. She was tired of being afraid.

"Get out of the fucking car, I said!" Robbie unlocked the driver's side door and simultaneously pushed Grace onto the cement. He crawled out after her and began punching her arms and chest. She couldn't move.

"Robbie, STOP IT!" She was crying and tossing her head from side to side, as he sat on top of her and continued to pummel her fragile body.

"You are such an ugly . . . dirty . . . filthy piece . . ." That was all Grace would remember, as she blacked out.

When she came to, she was in a hospital bed. Robbie sat beside her with a bouquet of fresh peach roses in his hand, that he bought from the flower shop in the lobby. His right eye was bruised from where she had scratched him, and his clothes were blood spattered. When the doctor asked what had happened, Robbie told him about the terrible car accident they were just in. Grace had been driving. Her parents were called, but they were vacationing in Florida.

"G-E-T . . . O-U-T!" Grace screamed at Robbie. She started to lift her left arm, but it was bandaged. Robbie quickly put his hand over her mouth.

"Shut up! Would you rather I killed you, bitch?" Robbie whispered, as he put the roses on the nightstand. "And don't try to move that arm, it's broken."

Grace sat back and closed her eyes. She wished she *had* died.

Chapter 28 - The Apartment

Grace spent the next couple of weeks in her apartment. She called her professors and informed them that she wouldn't be in class due to the terrible car accident she had been in. She asked them if they could leave the homework under her door and she would pick it up at night. Grace didn't want anyone to see her. She contacted her boss at the dry-cleaning store and told him the same story. Her mother and father were still in Florida, so she called Jesse and told her that she needed time off to study for a big exam.

Within these two weeks, Grace started to have problems sleeping at night. She was afraid Robbie would beat her door down, so she crawled next to the night-light and rocked herself to sleep against the window in her bedroom. The glow from the socket gave her a peaceful feeling. She could see the layout of the room and she felt better. Being alone in complete darkness frightened her.

I'm going mad, she thought, when she woke up one morning clutching the white teddy bear that Dan had given her on that Christmas Eve, so long ago, when he asked her to marry him. She sat for a minute, alone in her bedroom, and thought about him. She thought how different her life would have been if she had married him. She would never know the way a punch felt. She would never have to worry about whether she could have children or not. Her life would have been so uncomplicated.

Grace showered and dressed. The bruises were hardly noticeable by now. She applied her usual makeup and brushed her shoulder length hair. She missed her mother and father, and decided to stop by and say hello. They had gotten back from Florida just a day ago, and had left several messages on Grace's answering machine. "Hi, this is Grace. If you can't reach me here that means I'm probably at school, or at work. I'll call you back as soon as I can. Thanks for calling."

Grace left the message to give her parents the impression that she was busy studying, should they call. She wanted to make sure the bruises had healed before she saw them. She didn't want them to worry.

Grace walked down the back steps and outside to the parking lot. As she opened her car door, she glanced both ways to make sure nobody was around. She got into her 1984 black Ford Escort and drove down the hill and into the empty street.

As she drove toward her parents' house, her mind wandered. She wanted so badly to tell her parents everything and let them take over, and for them to hug her and tell her that he would never hurt her again. But she was afraid. Every time she tried to escape, he would find her. He had made threats to her about ruining her mother's business and she didn't know what to do about it. There were times in the past when he would harass Grace in her mother's office and then throw cans of Coca-Cola all over the walls, laughing all the while, splattering the pictures, and marking up the painted walls. Grace would have to stay late to clean it up, making sure not to leave any traces of Robbie's wrath. She didn't know what the next step would be. If she told anyone, he would kill her. If she went back to him, he would kill her. She was trapped.

Turning down her familiar street, she saw her parents' cars in the driveway. Her eyes filled with tears. As she pulled into the driveway, her mother opened the front door and ran outside to see her. She was crying.

"Oh Grace! Thank God you're all right!" her mother sobbed.

"Mom, what's the matter? Are you okay?"

"I just saw on the news that a girl from Quincy was beaten and killed by an ex-boyfriend. They didn't give the name of the girl . . . and your father and I have tried calling you, but you're never there, and we thought that Robbie had . . ." Grace's mother stopped talking and embraced her hard. Moments later, Grace's father came outside. He, too, had been crying.

"Mom, Dad, I'm fine. I've been busy at school. That's all. Look at me. I'm *fine.*" Grace started to get choked up and the three went inside. Grace and her parents talked for hours about school, her job and how much she loved her apartment. When they asked if she had seen Robbie, she lied. She didn't want to tell them about the incident on the hill. She didn't want to remember.

Before leaving, her mother gave her two bags of groceries, and her father slipped her a twenty-dollar bill in her pocket. She kissed them good-bye and promised to come back in a few days. On the way home, Grace stopped at the local supermarket and bought an Easter lily for her mother, with part of the twenty dollars that her father just gave her. She would bring it over during the week.

As Easter Sunday came, Grace dressed in the pale pink suit that her mother had bought her, and met her parents, grandparents, Richard, and Mary at church. She was a few minutes behind schedule, and when she arrived, they were already seated. She snuck in behind them and kissed her father on the cheek. As she listened to the priest, she asked God for the strength to help her get out of this deadly situation.

Throughout the day, Grace and her family talked about school, her jobs, and about Richard and Mary's wedding that was approaching the following month. Grace was the Maid of Honor, and she had become fast friends with Mary throughout the year. She looked forward to walking down the aisle. She hoped that someday, she too, would walk down the aisle. Grace wanted to forget the past and present and look to the future; a future in which Robbie was not a part.

That night, Grace talked to her mother a few times on the phone, and then went to bed. At one-thirty in the morning, she awoke to the sound of her doorbell buzzing. Grace stumbled to the intercom, next to the apartment door. "Uh, hello? Who is it?" she asked wearily.

"Grace, let me in!" It was Robbie. He was hollering and she could hear him pulling on the glass entrance door.

"Go away. It's late and I have nothing to say to you!" Grace yelled back into the intercom.

"If you don't let me in, so help me, I'll knock this door down!"

"Robbie, you'll wake the neighbors. Go home!"

Grace walked back into her bedroom and slipped back under the covers. As she closed her eyes, the buzzer sounded again. It started with a few short taps, and quickly turned into one long boisterous tone. She knew the neighbors would wake up, and she ran back to the intercom. She pressed the 'Listen' button and the buzzing stopped, although Robbie was still pressing the buzzer. *Oh, I cannot hold this stupid thing all night!* Grace thought as she heard Robbie cursing downstairs.

"Robbie, stop buzzing. Somebody will call the cops on you, you know," Grace said, almost laughing.

"Why are you such a baby?"

Grace was furious. She felt safe behind the apartment door, and at one-forty-five in the morning, she didn't particularly care if he was mad at her or not.

"Fine, you bitch! I'll go, but just pray that you see me before I see you, because I'll kill you!" Robbie shrieked, as she heard the door slam.

She released the button on the intercom and went back to bed. A few minutes later she heard the buzzer sound again. She looked out the window and saw Robbie driving away. *What in God's name is going on?* After getting out of bed for the third time, she listened at the intercom again. She heard no voices, only the same irritating buzzing sound from the entrance lobby. *He's jammed my doorbell,* she fumed. Holding her finger on the listen button, the noise stopped, but when she released it, it rang loud and filled her apartment. If she let go of the button and ran downstairs, she would wake all the neighbors. If she held the button down, she would be up all night until someone opened their door the next morning. At two o'clock, she heard someone walking up the back stairs. With one hand on the button, and one hand on the door, she opened it to see Raul, the man who lived across from her.

"Raul! Oh, thank God you're here," Grace whispered. Then she noticed he had been drinking, as he smiled when he turned to see her in a pink satin negligee.

"Well, hello . . . don't you look smashing!" he slurred.

"Listen, Raul. I need you to go down to the lobby and un-jam my buzzer. I've been standing here for over thirty minutes."

Raul was in his late thirties. He was Mexican, and wore a thick mustache, curled down at the corners of his mouth. His hair was black, and he slicked it back behind his ears. He always wore polyester suits to the clubs in town, and several gold necklaces hung from his small frame. He wore Brut cologne and carried a knife. Grace had seen it once before.

After a few minutes of staring, Raul went to the lobby and fixed her buzzer.

"Thank you, Raul. Now I can finally get some sleep," Grace said, as she closed the door.

The next day, Grace showered and dressed, and gathered up two dollars in quarters and went to the first floor laundry room to wash her clothes. As she put the detergent in the old machine, she heard voices from the lobby. She couldn't make them out and assumed they were friends of one of the other tenants. Twenty minutes went by and her clothes were ready to put into the dryer. As she packed the clothes in the dryer, she felt somebody watching her. She didn't want to look, out of fear, but did anyway. She was right.

"Robbie! How did you get in here?" Grace asked nervously. He was standing in the entranceway. It was the only way in or out of the room. Grace's eyes quickly darted around the room for something with which to defend herself, should he come up to her. The only thing she had were the keys to her apartment, in her pocket.

"Your pal, Raul, let me in. I told him I was your fiancé and he let me right in. Nice guy," Robbie laughed, as he moved closer to Grace. "You should've been paying more attention, Grace. I told you to watch your back, and here you are all alone in this dungeon."

Robbie grabbed Grace's arm as she raised it to hit him, and smacked her hard across the side of her head. She suddenly got dizzy and leaned against the washing machine, holding her head.

Grace started to cry. "Why can't you just leave me alone? Why don't you go back to Melissa and screw up *her* life?" She was so frustrated. She would never escape him, and it petrified her to think what he might do next.

"Because, Babe, I want to screw up yours!" he laughed. "Boy, you really are pitiful. Look at you! You really are an ugly piece of shit, do you know that?" Robbie walked back toward the door, and shut it.

"Robbie, for God's sake. Don't you think you've hurt me enough? Let me go on with my life!" Grace cried, as she stood against the washer. Her head still ached and she knew that she couldn't let him rape her again.

"I'm not gonna hurt you, if you just do what I say. Now, come over here," Robbie said, as he motioned to the floor beside him. He had unzipped his pants and pulled open his boxer shorts, exposing himself.

Grace walked over to him, remembering the keys in her pocket, and knelt before him. She reached into her left pant pocket and quietly took out her keys. "Close your eyes, Robbie, I want to do this right!" she whispered.

"That's my girl!" Robbie said, as he closed his eyes and put his hands on her head, pulling her toward him.

Grace pulled down his pants and slowly worked down his boxers. "Oh, Honey, I want to do this right!" she said, in a soft seductive tone. When his shorts were around his ankles, she began to kiss his thighs. It had to appear genuine. As she distracted him with her mouth, her hands were untying his sneaker laces and retying them together. Robbie's eyes were still closed.

When she was sure they were tied tightly, she took the keys from her lap, and held them in between her fingers. "What do you think of this?" Grace said, as she jabbed at his organ in one clean stroke, causing blood to trickle onto the cement floor. As he opened his eyes, and screamed in pain, she pushed him backwards and he fell to the floor. Her heart was racing as she ran for the front door and flew up the stairs and out through the lobby. She would only have a few minutes before he would be behind her. Running to the parking lot, she reached her car and locked the doors. Grace sped off, unaware of what her next move would be.

Chapter 29 - Robbie's Revenge

Grace decided to go to class. She wanted to put this incident out of her head, if only for a little while. *What was I thinking?* She whispered to herself as she pulled into the school parking lot. *He'll kill me for sure!* Grace didn't know what had made her do what she did. All she knew was how mad he made her. She didn't want to be a victim anymore. She didn't want to end up a statistic. Yet every time she tried to escape, to run away, he found her and hurt her worse. Not this time. She would stay in school until dark, go home and pack some of her clothes, and run away. She didn't know where she would go, but she knew that if she didn't get away soon, she wouldn't live to see twenty-three.

Grace spent the day looking over her shoulder as she went from class to class. At three-forty-five, she walked down the hall toward the lounge, where she and Jerry used to study. She thought about sitting by the window on one of the couches. She would curl up in the corner with one of her textbooks, and try to forget about the day's events. Maybe she could concentrate on school.

As Grace walked toward the back of the lounge, she heard a familiar voice call to her. When she turned around nervously, she saw Shawn waving frantically at her.

"Grace! Hey Grace!" he said, as he motioned her to come over.

Grace smiled and shook her head, as she walked toward him. "Shawn, hi! How've you been?" She hadn't talked to Shawn since that bitter December 26th, last year, when she found out that Robbie had cheated on her. She quickly remembered the conversation between them, and suddenly felt embarrassed.

"I've been okay. I just started here this past semester. Hopefully, I'll get into the College of Management next semester, but for now I'm taking Liberal Arts," Shawn said with disappointment in his voice.

Grace touched his arm and felt the hard muscle beneath his cotton jersey. "That's great! I can't believe you're going here now. Maybe we'll run into each other now and then. I'm taking business classes, too," Grace said, as they walked toward a table in the back of the lounge. As they sat, Grace looked at him in a serious manner.

"Shawn, I want to apologize for the way I behaved last December. God, I feel like a fool talking about it. I mean . . . when I hung up, I was crying and you must've thought I was an idiot!" Grace said with a distant look on her face, as if she were reliving it again.

Shawn touched her hand, and held it. "Grace, you had every right to respond that way. Robbie was your fiancé and he cheated on you. He's such a jerk! I mean, look at you! You're beautiful . . . and you're sweet," Shawn said softly, and withdrew his hand, shyly.

"Thanks, Shawn," Grace said and bowed her head.

"You are very welcome," Shawn said with a grin. "And as far as Robbie goes, he and Melissa can rot in hell for all I care. You should see those two at work. They're disgusting!"

"What do you mean?" Grace asked. Her stomach began to knot and she didn't know why, until Shawn continued.

"Well, ever since you and he broke up, he's been flaunting her in everyone's face. On top of that, he had the nerve to invite me to some cookout at her place. I think it's in a few weeks, when the weather gets hotter. Yeah, like I'd even consider it," Shawn said, as he looked distantly toward the glass window to his left. He was staring at the sun and quickly turned his head when his eyes started to water. He noticed Grace's reaction. *Didn't she know?* He thought nervously. Grace's eyes had begun to tear.

"Shawn, are you telling me that they are still together?" Grace said, as she brushed a tear away before it fell down her cheek.

"Oh Grace, I did it again, didn't I?" he said with hurt in his voice.

"Well, the thing is, after I talked to you in December, I called off the engagement. I gave his ring back and everything! Then I moved out of my house, just to get away from the whole situation, and also so that he wouldn't bother me anymore. Well, he finds out where I live, tells me that he loves me and gives me back my ring!" Grace noticed that Shawn was sitting with his mouth wide open. "Wait! There's more. So, I take the ring—No, I didn't wear it or anything, but I took it back. Now . . . for the past five or so months, he's been over all the time, following me back and forth to work and school, and busting into my apartment when I'm by myself. He won't leave me alone, and now you're telling me that he's been with Melissa all along?" Grace was flabbergasted, and exhausted from rehashing her life.

"Grace, he's sick!" Shawn said, disgusted. "I can't believe he's been doing that. Melissa was bragging that they're gonna get married next year. She doesn't have a ring or anything, but she sure talks like it."

Grace couldn't believe it. She wanted to confront Melissa. She wanted her to know everything that Robbie had done to her and let her know how petrified he had made her over the past few years. Grace was also furious, and couldn't believe that he was sleeping with another woman, while he was at the same time raping *her.* She wondered how he would explain the slice on his private part to Melissa. What could he possibly say to her? Grace started to laugh.

"Grace, what's so funny? Just a minute ago, you were crying. Are you all right?" Shawn asked, as he moved his chair closer to her.

"Oh Shawn, I was just thinking about something I did to Robbie today. He trapped me in my laundry room, and when he started to get a little . . . rough, I jabbed him you-know-where, with my apartment keys, and then I ran! I came right here." Grace thought back to the morning's events, and stopped laughing. "Oh my God, he's gonna be so furious. What if he finds me?"

"Grace, will he hurt you?" Shawn asked, obviously concerned.

"Um . . . no," Grace said, unconvincingly.

"I'm taking you home. You can pack some clothes and stay with me for a few days until he cools down. We can drive into school together tomorrow and pick up your car."

Grace sat for a few minutes. She was pondering what Shawn had just suggested. *Where else could she go?* She knew that Robbie would go to her apartment looking for her, and then to her parent's house if she wasn't there. Grace didn't want her parents to have to deal with him all night. But no, she couldn't impose on Shawn like this. It wasn't his problem.

"Thank you, Shawn, but I think I'll just go home tonight. I really don't feel right about imposing on you. And don't tell me that it's not an imposition, because it is."

"Grace, it's not a problem at all. C'mon, I don't feel right about you going home by yourself."

Shawn was worried about her. He wanted to pick her up and just hold her tight. He wanted to tell her how he felt about her. How much he had cared for her since the minute he saw her, but she was too vulnerable right now. The timing wasn't right.

"Shawn, I'll be fine, honestly," Grace said in a whispered tone, as she patted his hand.

"Well, at least let me drive you home. I'll make sure you get there all right and then, if you want, I'll come over tomorrow morning and pick you up for school. That way, your car won't be in the driveway and he'll think you're not home," Shawn said, as he stood and collected his book bag and Grace's texts.

"Okay, you've sold me. Thanks again, Shawn," Grace said, as she grabbed her pocketbook and threw it over her shoulder. "What a guy!" she said with a laugh, as they left the lounge.

When they reached Grace's apartment, Shawn shut the car off, walked around to the passenger door, and opened it for her. She got out of the car and they walked side by side to the back entrance door.

"Shawn, I can't thank you enough. Really! I'm glad I ran into you today," Grace said, as she leaned over and gave him a hug.

Shawn responded to her hug and hugged her back. As she pulled away and opened the door, she turned back to him. "Thanks again," she said.

"No problem. I'll see you tomorrow?" Shawn asked. He was tapping his foot nervously on the cement walkway. His hands were hidden in his jean pockets.

"Yup," Grace said, and walked through the door.

"Wait!" Shawn said, as he grabbed the door before it shut. Leaning toward Grace, he kissed her cheek. Grace closed her eyes.

"What was that for?" Grace asked softly.

"I just think you're a really sweet person, and I wanted you to know. That's all," Shawn said shyly. "Um . . . I'll see you in the morning. Bye," Shawn said, as he hurried to his car.

Grace watched him drive off, and walked up the back stairs and into her apartment. Once inside, she locked the door and went into her bedroom. It was just six o'clock and it was still light outside, but Grace changed into her emerald green satin nightshirt. She wanted to get comfortable, sit in bed with the pillows propped, and read her notes from class.

From the shrubs alongside the back parking lot, Robbie watched Shawn and Grace. He waited until Shawn drove off and then he walked toward the front door. He rang Raul's buzzer.

Raul, reaching for his jacket, heard the buzzing through his intercom, and responded. "Hey man, who is it?" he asked.

"Raul, pal, it's Robbie. Grace's fiancé," Robbie said in a friendly manner.

"Aw man, don't tell me you and your old lady are fightin' again," Raul said with a laugh, as he checked his hair in the mirror across the hall.

"Well, yeah. I was hoping . . . can you just buzz me in and I'll tell you?" Robbie said.

"Sure. Come on up, man," Raul said, as he buzzed him in and opened his apartment door. Raul was headed out on a date. He had heard Grace and Robbie arguing before, but he didn't want to interfere. He figured it wasn't his business what they did.

When Robbie reached the third floor, he spotted Raul locking his door. "Thanks, buddy. Hey, you headed out?" Robbie asked.

"Yeah, got myself a woman," Raul snickered.

"Well, before you go, can you just knock on her door, and say it's you? She won't even come to the door if she knows it's me! You know how women are," Robbie said with a laugh.

Raul said shook his head. "Man, I don't know what you've done, but you should've at least brought flowers or something," Raul said, as he knocked on Grace's door.

Grace was snuggled up in her bed, reading over her notes, when she heard someone knocking on her door. She jumped. Then she got out of bed and looked out the window. She didn't see Robbie's car. *Whew, not him,* Grace thought. "Who is it?" she asked, reaching for her silk robe.

"Raul," he said, turning toward Robbie and smiling. "You know, man, I don't want to be involved in your arguments anymore. You gotta shape up, man."

"Hold on Raul," Grace said, as she tied the sash on her robe and reached for the doorknob.

Just then, Raul patted Robbie on his back. "Good luck, man," he said, and flew down the back stairs.

When Grace opened the door, she flinched.

"Hi Babe," Robbie said, as he pushed the door open, while Grace tried unsuccessfully to shut it. "So," he started, "how long have you been screwing Shawn?"

Robbie was in the apartment now. He pulled her hand away from the doorknob, and slammed it hard. Then he grabbed Grace by the hair and tossed her from the entranceway into the living room. She fell against the oak coffee table. As she jumped up and approached him, he kicked her left leg on the outer thigh, and she fell again.

"Robbie, Shawn and I are friends. I ran into him at school today," Grace hollered, as she rubbed her thigh. When she tried to stand up this time, Robbie reached for the kitchen chair and threw it at her.

"Stay there, you slut!" he screamed. His face was red and he was sweating. The chair hit Grace's back and she couldn't move. She tried, but it hurt too much. "Robbie, stop it! Just S-T-O-P it!" she cried.

From what Grace could hear, Robbie was in her bedroom. She heard drawers opening and papers flying. *Got to stop this!* Grace thought, as she leaned on her left arm to force herself up. She limped on her right leg into her bedroom where she saw every drawer on the floor and papers ripped up all over her bed. "Robbie, those are my notes from class! Stop it!" she cried, as he tore them to shreds. "What are you *doing?"*

Robbie laughed as he threw the tattered notebook on the bed. "Where are the love notes, huh?" he yelled, as he kicked at the empty dresser drawer on the floor.

"Robbie, you'll never find anything because we're just friends! You, on the other hand, have been fooling around for months!" Grace hollered, and then hobbled out of the room, before he hit her again.

Robbie ran after her and followed her into the kitchen. "You *bitch!* You have the nerve to accuse *me,* when *you've* been the one screwing around!" Robbie said, as he grabbed Grace's arms and shook her hard. Then, he added, "I took this back, too, you slut! You don't deserve it anymore." Robbie pulled her engagement ring out of his pocket and flashed it in her face.

"Robbie, give me that back!" Grace had decided months ago that she would return it to the jewelers and get her money back, so she could pay off her charge card.

"No way!" Robbie responded, as he pushed Grace away from him. Robbie opened the refrigerator door and reached for the orange juice. He laughed as he dumped it on the kitchen floor.

"Robbie, please just go. Leave me alone. You can keep your stupid ring!" Grace sat on the living room floor and watched as he continued to pull food out of her refrigerator and throw it on the floor. She knew that if she attempted to stop him, he would just hit or kick her. She would clean it up later.

Before he left the kitchen, he pulled some of the cabinet drawers out and they made a heavy thud when they reached the floor. Silverware was scattered amongst the tomatoes, milk and orange juice.

Robbie walked over to Grace, who was sitting motionless on the living room floor, watching his destruction. "What's the matter, slut!" Robbie laughed, as he slapped the top of her head. Grace reached up with her right hand and grabbed him. She pulled his arm so hard that he fell on the floor next to her. Grace jumped up and kicked him between his legs, and turned to run for the door.

"You b-i-t-c-h!" he yelled, as he kicked his foot out, catching the back of her leg, and causing her to stumble. As she gathered herself back up, Robbie snatched at her nightshirt, ripping the seam of her shirttail, and pulling Grace backwards toward him.

"You just don't . . . let . . . up, do you?" Robbie said, winded from the kick. He dragged Grace by her hair into the kitchen and flung her to the wet floor. Once again, she started to get up, but Robbie kicked her left thigh again, where he had kicked her earlier. She fell back on the floor, her nightshirt soaked with juice.

"Bravo! Bravo! Where's the camera when you need one?" Robbie said with a laugh, as he clapped loudly. "You would have been one terrific actress, Grace."

"Go to hell," Grace whispered.

"Excuse me? Did you say something?" Robbie mocked, as he looked around the kitchen, curiously. "Ah, here they are," he said, reaching for the steak knives Grace's mother had given her for Christmas last year. Robbie pulled out the largest one and threw himself on top of Grace's stomach, tearing her nightshirt down the middle with the knife. He sat up and pulled at the clothing, until she lay naked beneath him.

"Now, I suggest you do what I say," Robbie said, as he leaned into her left ear, licking it with his tongue.

"Robbie, why are you doing this? I know that you have Melissa . . . that you've been with her all along. I don't care! Why don't you just get off me, and go see *her*?" Grace said in as calm a voice as she could muster.

"You think I'm gonna *do* you? No . . . this is punishment!" Robbie said. His face had become distorted, almost mad-like, as he grabbed her hands and pinned them down with his right hand. He began to look around at the floor. "Okay," he said, as he reached for the brown leather knife cover, "we're ready to begin!"

Grace started to toss back and forth beneath him, trying to shake him off of her. Robbie dropped the knife and punched her face with his left hand. Her mouth and nose started to bleed, and she turned her head to the side. She began to scream.

"I *told* you to do what I say, you stupid bitch!" Robbie said, as he jumped on her stomach. He picked the knife back up and held it to her throat. Grace flinched. "Do you want me to do this?" Robbie asked.

"Robbie, I'm sorry. Please . . . put the knife down! Please . . ." Grace was crying louder.

"S-h-u-t up, you baby!" Robbie said. "Now . . . I've tried everything I could think of to get through to you, but you haven't changed. You've been cheating on me since we started dating, and I think it's time I got even!" Robbie was still sweating, and his hand was shaking. He looked into Grace's eyes, and then spit on her face. Grasping the knife tighter, he placed it against her throat again, harder than before, causing a small line of blood to trickle down her neck.

After a minute or two of holding the knife to her, and seeing the terror in her eyes, he reached for the holder and placed the knife in it. Before Grace could move, he thrust the handle of the knife into her exposed vagina. He had positioned himself off her stomach and onto her legs, so that she couldn't kick him. Grace's hands were free, however, and she reached toward him to slap him.

"Stop hitting me!" he yelled.

"Robbie, please . . . it hurts!" Grace cried, as she watched his hands work the five-inch handle. The leather case was rubbing against her tender flesh, as she felt something sticky escape her. A small pool of blood had gathered beneath her.

Grace continued to punch and scream. She prayed that someone would hear her and help. But nobody came. Grace stopped crying and concentrated on the bottom of the stove. She noticed how dirty it was. She decided that she would clean it tomorrow.

When Robbie finished her punishment, he pulled himself up by the handle of the kitchen cabinet. Grace rolled over into a fetal position and began to whimper. Robbie spit on her, walked into the bathroom, grabbed a dirty face cloth from the hamper, and tossed it to her.

Then he laughed, and walked out.

Chapter 30 - Robbie Gets Caught

During the following two weeks, Grace studied for finals. When she ran into Shawn in the library at school, he confronted her.

"Grace, where have you been? I've been calling you, but you won't return my calls, and when I stopped by that day, you never opened the door. What's going on?" Shawn demanded.

"Leave me alone, okay?" Grace whispered, as she gathered up her books and walked out of the library.

"Grace," Shawn continued, when he caught up with her, "don't shut me out. I know something is going on. Let me in. I care about you," Shawn said, as he turned her face toward him.

"Shawn, I don't deserve you to care about me. Believe me! You don't know the *half* of what's been going on in my life, and I certainly don't want to tell you now!" Grace turned her face away again, and stared blankly at the rust-colored tile beneath her feet.

"Grace, I'm worried about you. Please . . . just talk to me." Shawn was looking at Grace and stroking her hair. Grace closed her eyes, and began to tremble.

"C'mon, let's go sit somewhere," Shawn said, as he took her hand.

"Shawn, I need to get through this alone. I can't depend on anyone to get me through it. Please understand. I need to do this alone," Grace said, as she kissed his cheek and said good-bye.

On the following Saturday, Grace prepared for her brother's wedding. She would wear an emerald green taffeta dress, fitted at the waist, and full on the bottom. That morning, Grace, along with her mother and a few other bridesmaids, went to the hair salon to get coiffured. Her hair was pulled up in a twist with tiny curls around her face.

They spent the morning talking about the wedding, wondering if the flowers would be set up properly, if Richard would be on time, etc. They laughed and joked about married life, and told Mary how happy they were that she was becoming a part of the family.

That afternoon, as Grace drove back to her apartment to get dressed, she remembered the conversation with Shawn about Melissa talking about marriage. *I have to call her,* she thought.

Entering her apartment, she tossed her pocketbook on the kitchen table and picked up the beige wall phone next to the refrigerator. Dialing information, she waited for the operator. "Yes . . . could I have the number for a Strolka . . . Melissa, in Boston . . . please." Grace's hands shook and her palms were sweaty. *Why am I warning her? He cheated on me with her, for God's sake!* Grace thought, as she heard the operator connect her. The phone rang twice before a man answered.

"Hello, Strolka residence." His voice was deep. *Another boyfriend?* Grace wondered.

"Yes . . . I . . . uh, was looking for Melissa. Is she there?" Grace's forehead was forming tiny beads of sweat.

"Yeah, hang on . . . Sis, telephone."

Grace listened as she heard the man, apparently her brother, call for her.

"Hello." It was Melissa. Grace froze. She suddenly felt awkward dialing the *other woman.* She wanted to hang up, but it was too late for that.

"Hi, Melissa? This is Grace Preston," she said nervously.

"Well, well. What'd ya know? What do you want? Is Robbie back? Sorry, Grace, he's all mine now," Melissa said with a vicious laugh in her voice.

"Melissa, I called because I am on my way to my brother's wedding in a few hours, and I started thinking about something my friend said about you. He said that you were talking about getting married to Robbie next year, and I just wanted—"

Melissa interrupted. "Yeah, so what's your point?"

"Well," Grace continued, "I felt that I should let you know what's been going on over the past few months . . . please listen, and don't say anything until I'm done, because I don't think you'll believe it."

"Okay, I'll bite . . . what won't I believe?" Melissa asked in a mocking tone.

"Well, for starters, back in December when this whole thing happened, Robbie sent me three dozen roses and pleaded with me to take him back." Grace heard a gasp from the other end, and quickly continued. "Then, he kept coming over until I moved out. He found out where I lived and came over. He gave me my engagement ring back and asked me to marry him again."

"What the hell are you talking about?" Melissa fumed. "Robbie gave the ring back to the damn jewelry store and paid off the loan he took out. So you are full of shit!"

"Wait . . . don't hang up," Grace begged. "He made me put half of the cost of the ring on my charge card, so he doesn't owe anything on the ring. He gave it back to me months ago, but I told him I didn't want to marry him. Now, for the past several months he's been following me to work, school and waiting for me at my apartment. He's busted my front doorbell, and destroyed my apartment when he thought I was dating someone else. Melissa . . . he's been raping me for months, and when I try to stop him, he beats me up. I've been too afraid to tell anyone because he says he'll kill me, and even though I don't like you, I don't want to see you end up like that." Grace finished her speech, and waited for a response.

"Are you serious? He's been sleeping with the both of us all this time?" Melissa didn't seem to hear the word *rape*.

"No. He's been *raping* me." Grace said. Just then, she heard someone knocking on her door.

"Melissa, please don't hang up. Someone is at my door. Hang on," Grace said, as she put the phone down and began to open the door. It was Robbie. *Perfect timing,* she thought. Grace opened the door and let Robbie in. "Hi Robbie. Welcome to my home," she laughed. "Can you hold on for one minute? I just want to get my dress for the wedding." Grace went into her bedroom and grabbed the dress, picking up her shoes and pocketbook at the same time. When she came out, she saw that Robbie hadn't noticed the phone off the hook. He was sitting calmly on her couch.

"Grace, I know the wedding is today, and I don't want to bother you. I want you to know that I love you, and I'm sorry for what's been going on. I'm sorry for what happened a few weeks ago."

Grace stood by the opened door, and picked up the receiver. "Hello, are you still there?" she asked.

Melissa was yelling into the phone to let her speak to Robbie.

"Okay, hold on one second and I'll get him," Grace said, as she tossed the phone to Robbie. "Looks like this call is for you. I'll give you some privacy," Grace said, as she quickly closed the apartment door and ran down the stairs. She didn't wait for anything. She jumped into her car and drove as fast as she could to her parents' house. Nothing would ruin this wedding.

Her brother's wedding was exceptional. Everything was perfect. The flowers were placed on the altar, as planned, and Richard was on time. After Richard and Mary were married, and began to walk back down the aisle, Grace followed. When she reached her parents, she noticed her mother was laughing and crying at the same time.

"Psst...Mom, what's going on?" Grace whispered as she passed by.

"You've got the price tags on your shoes and when you knelt beside Mary, at the altar, everyone saw it!"

Grace had been in such a rush to get out of her apartment that she forgot to take the price tags off. They were only $9.99, too. She was so embarrassed, but laughed it off.

The reception was beautiful. Grace cried when her mother and brother danced, and again when Mary danced with her father. Grace was glad to have a *big sister*. She and Mary had become friends over the past few years, and she was glad that she and Richard were married. Mary had confronted Grace on numerous occasions when she had a black eye or fat lip. She knew Robbie's type, and she saw how introverted Grace had become since she first met her. Grace knew that Mary knew. She wanted to tell her, but she was too afraid.

After the wedding, Grace drove back to her apartment. She entered through the front door at 1:45 AM. When she reached her door, she pulled out the key and opened it.

"Oh, my God!" she exclaimed, when she saw her apartment. The floor plants had been thrown against the tan wall and the smell of dried mud filled the room. The walls were stained, the pictures of her family were tossed all over the apartment, and the oak table with glass partitions was key scratched.

Grace ran into her bedroom and gasped. Robbie was lying naked on top of her bed with her lingerie scattered all over the room. Her collection of teddy bears had been beheaded, and her dresser drawers had been torn apart.

"ROBERT. Get Up!" Grace screamed as loud as she could, startling Robbie. He jumped up, and rubbed his eyes.

"What are you doing here?" Grace demanded.

"I've been waiting for you," Robbie said as he stood up, reaching for his jeans that were tossed on the floor.

"What have you done to my apartment? You are going to clean this up!" Grace said, as she grabbed his arm.

Robbie grabbed back and punched her in the chest. She jerked backwards, but held her ground, defiantly. "Go ahead, hit me. I don't care! I want you out of my apartment . . . NOW!" Grace snapped. She lunged for Robbie and they both landed on the bed. She fell on top of him and started to hit his arms and chest, while screaming for him to leave her alone.

Robbie pushed up with his pelvis, and Grace rolled to the side, and then off the bed. As she started to get up, Robbie grabbed her right foot, and she fell on the floor. "You are not going anywhere, you dirty piece of shit. Listen to what I heard tonight while I waited for you," Robbie said, as he stepped on her to get to the answering machine. He pressed the *play* button, and sat back on the bed.

"Hi, Grace. It's Shawn. I know you're at the wedding. Hope its going okay. Listen, I just called to say that I really care about you . . . I really do, Grace." The message cut off.

"You w-h-o-r-e!" Robbie said, as he stood up to rewind the message and play it again.

"Robert, I am tired of this!" Grace barked, and pushed him into the nightstand.

After being afraid for the past two and a half years, Grace had had enough. She had lost her friends, her self-esteem, and maybe even the chance to have children someday. She had nothing left. Yes, she cared about Shawn, but she couldn't go on living this way. She tried to escape, and every time she did, Robbie found her. He threatened to kill her. He threatened to kill her family. Grace knew that she would never be *normal* again, even if she did survive this terror. But she didn't care anymore. If she couldn't kill him, she would die trying.

When Grace pushed him into the nightstand, she ran into the living room, knowing he would follow her. He did. As he chased her around her apartment, he knocked over the kitchen chairs and pulled up the sofa cushions. The apartment looked like a cyclone had struck it. Grace didn't care. She grabbed a knife out of the kitchen drawer and waved it in the air. Robbie stopped and stared.

"May God strike me dead, if I don't kill you tonight. I swear. If you don't leave me alone, I will kill you!" Grace was hysterical. Her eyes were wild, and her hair was wet and all around her face. She was still wearing the emerald green dress.

"Oh, tough guy!" Robbie mocked. He walked toward Grace and she jabbed the knife at him.

"Don't come near me!" Grace growled. "I am tired of living in fear. I am tired of you running my life and I can't take it anymore!" She began to cry, and her hands were shaking. Robbie took this opportunity to run up on her and take the knife away from her. Suddenly, he was now holding the large knife.

"Who's in control *now*, huh?" he said, waving the knife in Grace's direction.

"Tell you what," he said, as he kicked her in the knee, causing her to fall on the kitchen floor, "if you think it's so bad, why don't you kill yourself. 'Cause that is the only way you're gonna get out of this relationship . . . unless, of course, I kill you first." Robbie had the knife pointed at Grace's neck.

Grace turned her head and caught a glimpse of herself in the hall mirror. She was on her hands and knees. Her hair was a mess. Her eyes were swollen from crying. She knew that she would be like this for the rest of her life, however long that would be. *No!* She thought. *I will NOT end up a statistic!* Her life flashed before her as she thought of her family, her long-lost friends, her God. She had prayed so many times for Him to give her the strength to live through this misery. She had prayed countless times in the quiet of her room for God to save her.

Grace took one hand off the floor and pushed Robbie as hard as she could against the kitchen cabinets. He dropped the knife and she kicked it away. The next ten minutes or so they fought on the kitchen floor. Robbie punched her face and ripped at her flesh with his fingernails. He kicked her chest, and she fell back. Robbie was pulling her hair out in clumps and throwing them on top of her. Her dress was ripped. Her mouth and nose were bleeding. Robbie grabbed for the knife and sliced her left knee and wrist before she kicked it out of his hand.

And still, nobody called for help.

Grace proceeded to kick his back and legs, as he struggled to get off the floor. He kicked her left leg and she stumbled. Robbie ran into the bathroom and grabbed the metal pole that holds the shower curtain, and yanked it out of the wall. He lunged for Grace and released the rod. The pole hit her in the chest, and she started to bleed. As Grace screamed out, Robbie, looking at her frantically, ran out of the apartment.

Chapter 31 - Grace's Fight Back

Grace awoke the following morning covered in dried blood. She struggled to get up and limped toward the bathroom. As she passed the kitchen, she thought of how she had almost lost her life last night. She noticed her left knee, cut deeply by the knife wound. Her chest still pounded. She felt her face and winced. When she saw her reflection in the mirror, she began to cry—a muffled, whimpering animal-like sound.

"Oh God . . . what has happened to me . . . oh dear God, why?" she cried, blotting her face with a cold face cloth.

Grace knew what she had to do.

* * *

Mary and Richard had decided to go to Martinique for their honeymoon. They would be back in seven days. She needed to talk to Mary about her situation. Mary had always appeared to be independent and strong—qualities that Grace admired. She needed to confide in her, tell her everything. She was tired of going it alone. She was ready to make a change.

Grace remained in her apartment for the remaining seven days. She spent each day cleaning up the debris from the fight. She told her parents that she was going to spend a few days with some friends from college, and they thought it was a wonderful idea.

Grace stayed in her apartment and cried herself to sleep every night. She locked the apartment door and put the kitchen table up against it. She stacked the kitchen chairs on top of the table for extra support. Her body was sore and she had dark purple bruises all over her. She was in a lot of pain.

On the morning of her brother's return from his honeymoon, Grace cleaned her face and covered the bruises as best she could, and drove to her parents' house. When she arrived, she checked herself in the rearview mirror, and made a sign of the cross. Richard and Mary were already there. As she walked into the house and down the stairs, she saw that her mother was sitting beside Mary and her father was holding a glass in his hand.

"Ah, you're just in time for my toast," her father said with a smile.

Mary looked up and saw the expression on Grace's face. She was smiling but her eyes were teary.

"Welcome home, you guys! How was the honeymoon?" Grace asked, as she looked directly at Mary.

Mary was extremely perceptive, and smart. Grace could tell that she knew something was wrong. "Will you excuse me for a minute? I want to talk to Grace about something," Mary said, as she got off the brown tweed sofa and started walking toward Grace.

"Honey, is everything all right?" her mother asked.

"Um...yeah. I just really need to talk to Mary." Grace's eyes were watery now, and her face felt flushed. Mary put her arm around her and they walked into the kitchen on the other side of the house.

"Grace, I knew something was up the second you walked in. Is it Robbie?" Mary asked once they were alone.

Grace started to cry. "Mary, I know I should've told somebody sooner, but I was so afraid. I thought he was going to kill me. He's made threats before and he's threatened to kill Mom and Dad before too. He even had plans to take money from Mom's business! I don't know what to do anymore, but I can't go on like this." Grace was crying louder now.

"Grace, take a deep breath, and tell me where he is right now," Mary said, taking Grace's hand.

"He's . . . he's probably at work right now. He works until eleven tonight," Grace whimpered.

"Grace, we're going right now to the police station. You are going to file for a 209A—it's a restraining order. It is the only way you can get him out of your life."

She looked curiously at Mary. *How did she know so much about this stuff?* Grace wondered. Mary continued, "I'll go with you if you want me to. Your parents can go or not. It's up to you. You know, you're taking a big step by telling someone. It's not your fault that he's done these things to you, no matter what he says. You are not to blame."

"But, he took my virginity away. How can another man ever love me?" Grace asked.

"Oh, Grace. Believe me, there is a man somewhere in this world that will love you as you are. You are not dirty because Robbie did what he did."

"But Mary, you don't understand. Nobody can ever love me after everything that Robbie has done." Grace's face was wet with tears, and she was out of breath.

"Look, Grace, Robbie is a monster. He is a filthy piece of garbage! You were strong enough to come home and ask for help. I want to help you. Get your pocketbook and let's go tell your parents. I think they should know what's going on." Mary gave Grace a hug, kissed the top of her head, and stood up.

"And for the record, Grace . . . I once dated a man a lot like Robert. Believe me . . . you're doing the right thing." Mary's eyes were brimming with tears, as she continued. "See, I know you'll be okay, because I thought the same thing. 'Nobody will want me if they knew what happened,' and then I met your brother."

Grace stared at Mary for a minute or so, and took her hand. "I'm so sorry, I had no idea. You seem so strong and independent."

"Time—you need time to get through this. Time to heal . . . you'll be okay, Grace."

A few minutes later, Mary and Grace emerged from the kitchen.

"Mom, Dad . . . Richard. Mary and I are going to the police station. I'm getting a restraining order against Robbie." Grace stood next to Mary as she held her hand. Her parents looked dumbfounded, and stood with their mouths open.

"Honey . . . are you okay? What did he do to you? You can tell us," her mother cried. She turned to her husband. "Jack, I *told* you that boy was no good! I don't understand why nobody will listen to me!"

Her brother sat on the sofa and didn't move. He didn't know what to do or say.

"Jack, get my pocketbook. I'm going with them," she said, as she moved closer to Grace and hugged her.

"Mom, I think I'd like just Mary to go." Grace knew this would hurt her mother's feelings, but she trusted Mary to help her through this. She didn't want her parents to hear the gory details about the battering anyway.

"Honey, I love you. I want to go!" Her mother's voice reflected the hurt that her eyes expressed.

"Okay," Grace said, as she started up the stairs.

"Grace, would it be okay if I come too?" her father asked quietly.

"Yeah. Let's just go before I change my mind."

Chapter 32 - Section 209A

Grace's father drove, while her mother sat in the front seat and cursed the day she ever met Robbie. Mary and Grace sat in the back of the Lincoln Town Car, and said nothing.

When they arrived at the police station, a uniformed policeman behind the counter asked what the problem was.

"I would like to get a restraining order against my ex-fiancé," Grace responded softly to the officer.

"Okay, then. Go over to that telephone located on the wall. Pick it up and tell them what you told me." The officer finished his speech, and walked away.

Grace walked over toward the black telephone hanging on the pale yellow cement wall. She picked up the receiver.

"Precinct Five here, Officer O'Hare speaking. What can I do for you?" The voice on the other end was raspy. He had a Boston accent.

"I . . . I would like to file for a restraining order," Grace said meekly.

"Who is the offender?" the voice asked.

"He is my ex-fiancé," Grace replied. She was looking at Mary as she answered the man's questions.

"Would you be willing to take this matter to court, and face the offender directly, if need be?"

Grace took the receiver away from her mouth and told her family what Officer O'Hare had just asked. Mary nodded. "I'll go with you, Grace," she said.

Grace put the receiver up to her mouth again. "Yes, I will go to court," she said.

"Do you need a photographer tonight?" he asked.

"Yes . . . I will," Grace said, as she began to cry and handed the phone to her father.

"I'll be right down," Officer O'Hare responded.

Within minutes, two officers and one photographer came through the double doors. One officer, O'Hare, was about five-foot eleven, and had a muscular frame. He looked like he was in his early thirties. His black hair was short. His eyes were light brown. The other officer was older. He appeared to be in his late fifties and was shorter than Officer O'Hare. His hair was silver and he wore tinted glasses. The photographer was a woman. She was tall, thin and plain looking. She wore jeans and a beige cotton top. On her shoulder, she carried a camera and two camera bags.

"Excuse me, I'm her mother. Why is there a photographer here? Are we going to be in the newspaper?" her mother inquired innocently.

"No ma'am. We need to take pictures of your daughter's bruises, and any visible scars she may have. I'm sorry . . . Detective Salvagi." He extended his hand to Mrs. Preston. "I'm sorry about your daughter."

Mrs. Preston began to cry. "Honey, is it true? Do you have bruises on your body?"

Grace knew this was the reason why she didn't want her family to go with her. Mary could handle the truth, but she knew this would destroy her parents. Her father sat on the hard wooden bench and stared blankly at the ceramic tile beneath his feet.

"If you'll follow me, Miss Preston," Officer O'Hare said, as he led Grace into an office behind the double doors. Mary followed behind her, and then turned to her in-laws. "I don't think you'll want to be there for the picture taking. We'll be right out," she said, as she closed the doors.

While her parents waited in the hall, Grace was uncovering bruises and knife wounds. The one on her chest had turned yellow, while the one on her left thigh was five inches round and almost black. The photographer winced a few times out of sheer instinct, and snapped the pictures.

Mary held Grace's hand and helped her get dressed afterwards. She was a tower of strength.

After they had finished, Detective Salvagi asked her parents some questions in the adjoining office, while Officer O'Hare questioned Grace. For over an hour, she sat in a hard wooden chair and rehashed his beatings. When the interrogation had finished, Officer O'Hare reached for the telephone.

"Hello, Judge. Sorry to bother you on a Sunday night and all, but I have a 209A in front of me. Yes, the victim is here with her family, now . . . Yes, I've got pictures and a signed statement from her and her sister-in-law that he's been abusive for over two years . . . I'll set it up for tomorrow morning, sir. Thank you."

Grace was reunited with her parents and they all stood in front of Officer O'Hare's desk, waiting.

"What was all that about?" Grace asked, as he hung up the phone.

"That was Judge Carson. I called him at home. We are going to grant you an emergency restraining order, Miss. You will go into court tomorrow morning at ten o'clock, and he will hear both sides of the story. You have pictures. I will give those to the judge tomorrow morning when I see them. If your parents want to go, they are more than welcome to. And, I'm going to pick Mr. Gagnon up tonight. Is he at home?" Officer O'Hare finished talking and waited for an answer.

"No, he's at work for another few hours or so," Grace said, worriedly. "What happens now?" she asked.

"Well, I'll send one of my men down to pick him up. We'll serve him with the papers and we'll hold him for the night in detention. Tomorrow, we'll take him to court and the judge will decide what to do next. Most likely, he'll grant the restraining order, and Mr. Gagnon will not be able to come near you at work, school or at home." Officer O'Hare noticed the expression on Grace's face. She looked scared. "Don't worry, he won't hurt you again," he said, as he patted her arm.

That night, Grace slept in her old bed at home. She couldn't get much rest, but it was comforting to know that Robbie was off the streets, for now. When she woke up the next morning, her stomach was in knots. She would have to come face to face with him, in a court of law.

Grace showered and dressed. Looking around her old room, she reminisced about her younger days—the times before Robbie. She missed her diary. She missed her childhood. Now, at age twenty-two, when most girls her age were partying in college and playing the field, she was fighting for her life, hoping just to see another birthday.

"Mom, Dad . . . I'm ready," Grace said, as she combed her hair one last time. She had on a dark blue suit and white silk blouse. Her hair was combed straight, and she wore no jewelry.

"Honey, we're ready. We're just waiting for Mary and Richard to come over," her mother replied. Just then, the doorbell rang.

"Sorry we're late. Ready?" Mary asked, as she hugged Grace. Richard was in the car. He hadn't come the night before to the police station. He didn't know how to express his anger and hurt for his sister. Grace understood.

"Ready as I'll ever be," Grace said with a heavy sigh. Her parents followed shortly down the stairs, and her father closed and locked the door behind them. He had also been very quiet.

When they arrived, they spotted Robbie's car and his parents' car in the driveway. Grace looked away quickly and rubbed her stomach.

"You'll be fine, Grace. This is the only way to stop that crummy piece of dirt," Mary said.

"I know, I know. I'm just scared," Grace said.

Mr. Preston stopped the car and opened the doors for the ladies. He walked guardedly beside his daughter. Richard walked beside Mary, and Grace and her mother walked next to each other. When they got inside, they spotted Robbie and his family. He had brought three cousins, all of whom were lawyers, along with his parents, and his sister, Nancy.

"Oh my God!" Grace said in a loud whisper. "I can't believe he brought all those people!"

"Don't look at him," Mary said. "Concentrate on what you're going to say." Mary took a quick glance across the hall and Robbie was smirking at her. She shot him a look and turned away. *How dare he be so arrogant?*

Thirty minutes later, their names were called. Grace stood up. She felt weak.

"I can't believe it's come to this," she said, as her father escorted her into the judge's chambers.

It took only fifteen minutes for the judge to listen to both sides before he granted Grace the emergency restraining order.

"Judge, she's lying. I've never laid a hand on her. She's covering for her father! Her father's been beating her since she was five!" Robbie yelled.

Grace turned to Robbie and asked him why, why did he sink that low? She turned back to her father, whose face had lost all expression. He sat without saying a word, and just waited for the judge to speak.

When the judge had dismissed Robbie's information as ludicrous, Robbie continued to argue that Grace beat him up, and that he was just defending himself.

"Mr. Gagnon, will you stand up, please? And . . . Grace, you too." Judge Carson was about to make a point. "Thank you both. Now, Mr. Gagnon, you are how tall, six-two and weigh approximately one-ninety-five, am I correct?"

Robbie shook his head.

"And Grace, you are five-four and weigh about one hundred pounds, correct?"

Grace shook her head.

"Are you trying to tell me, Mr. Gagnon, that this little girl beats you up, and you sustain no injuries? You have no proof. But Grace, on the other hand, has sustained multiple sprains, bloody lips and noses, and vaginal scarring. Are you telling me that *you* are the victim here?" Judge Carson's voice was rising and his face was becoming red.

"Get out of my courtroom, Mr. Gagnon, before I throw you out myself. I see fit for an emergency restraining order and it will go into effect immediately. You, Mr. Gagnon, will not go within one hundred yards of Grace. You will not contact her in any way, shape or form. Do you understand me? And, if I find out that you have seen or contacted her, I will see you back in this courtroom, and next time, I won't be so nice! Good day!"

As Robbie and his family filtered out of the courtroom, Judge Carson spent a few minutes talking to Grace and her family. He assured them that he was the *toughest* judge in town, and he would see to it personally that justice was served.

Grace could finally feel safe. Or so she thought.

Chapter 33 - Robbie Defies the Order

When Grace got home that afternoon, there were seven hang-ups on her answering machine. As she got undressed, the phone rang.

"Hello," Grace said while she unbuttoned her silk blouse.

"Grace . . . Hi." It was Robbie.

"You know you can't talk to me. Leave me alone!" Grace slammed the phone down. The phone rang again.

Grace grew nervous all over again. "Hello," she said, this time more angrily.

"Grace, don't hang up. I just want to know why you did this to me? Why don't you want me near you?" Robbie was whispering into the phone, and Grace could barely hear him.

"Robbie, you know why. You've hurt me and I can't go on living in fear. I need to get my life back. I need to be free from you. Good-bye!"

Grace slammed the phone down on its cradle and then picked it up again. She kept slamming the phone against the edge of the base, until it shattered. She started to cry, and wondered if she had made the right decision.

Three weeks passed, in a daze. Grace thought about calling Shawn. *It's only eight o'clock at night so he should be home,* she thought. She dialed the number, and heard the ringing through the receiver.

"Hello, this is Shawn," he answered.

"Shawn . . . it's Grace." She missed his voice. Suddenly, she missed him.

"Grace! Is everything okay? I haven't heard from you in ages! I miss you," Shawn said.

"Yes. Actually, I'm feeling pretty fine. I wanted to know if . . . if you wanted to come over and hang out with me for a while."

"Why, is Robbie bothering you?" Shawn sounded worried. "Are you scared, Grace?"

"Oh, no! As a matter of fact, that's what I wanted to talk to you about," Grace said with a hint of mystery in her voice. Just then, Grace heard someone at her front door. "Hang on Shawn, someone is at my door. Probably the landlord looking for this month's rent," she said with a smile.

Grace rested the phone on her bed, and skipped to the front door. A few days ago, her father had installed a safety lock and chain on the door, above the factory installed lock. Grace unlocked the door, and opened it as wide as the chain would allow.

"No! Go away!" Grace screamed. It was Robbie. As she tried to shut the door, he stuck his foot in between the small opening in the doorway, and pushed hard. The chain snapped from the wall, and as he pushed harder, the area surrounding the lock on the wall collapsed. The door made a heavy thud as it fell to the floor. Grace ran into her room.

"Shawn, call the police! Tell them Robbie's here and—" The line went dead. Robbie had pulled the phone cord from the kitchen wall. Grace crawled into her closet in her bedroom and found a small spot beneath her winter sweaters to hide.

"Where are you, you little bitch?" Robbie hollered through the apartment. As he looked for her, he continued, "You know, Melissa has left me. Did you know that? Yup, she found out about the restraining order and she said that if I didn't leave her alone, she'd file for one, too. Can you believe it?" he said, almost laughing.

Grace sat perfectly still in her closet. She was sweating. She couldn't take another beating. Not tonight, not ever. Suddenly, she heard the sound of sirens in the distance.

Could they be coming to help me? Grace prayed. She prayed that the police would come and arrest him.

Robbie heard the sirens and looked out the picture window in the living room. "Shit . . . the cops! You've got it made, slut. You lucked out this time. But when I find you again, you're dead."

Suddenly all was quiet. Had he left? A few minutes later, the police arrived to find the door busted down, and the apartment in shambles. Officer O'Hare walked into the bedroom to find a quivering Grace, still hiding in the closet.

As he pulled her out, he hugged her. "It's all right. It's all right."

He gave her a heavy gray blanket to wrap herself in, forgetting that it was the middle of summer, and brushed her hair away from her eyes. "We've got him now, Grace. Breaking and entering. Attempted assault and battery. Breaking the 209A. He's through. He'll go to jail, now. He doesn't realize what he's done this time."

Within minutes, Shawn arrived. He flew up the back stairs and into Grace's apartment. When he found her in the bedroom, he ran up and gave her a long hug. He didn't let go. "Grace, it's okay. They'll get Robbie. Do you want to talk about it?"

Grace waved good-bye to the police officers, thanked them for coming, and turned back to Shawn. "No, Shawn, I don't think I do. Maybe someday, but for now just hold me, and don't ever let go."

Chapter 34 - Grace Moves Forward

Within seven days, Grace was called back into Judge Carson's chambers to discuss the most recent events. She hadn't told her parents about the incident. She knew how worried they had become over the past month or so, and didn't want to cause them any additional strain or stress.

When Shawn offered to go with her to the courthouse, she said, "No, I need to do this by myself. I need to face him alone." She needed to prove to herself that she was strong, and becoming stronger every day that he was out of her life.

That morning, she dressed in another suit, a red one this time. She curled her hair and put on a pair of black leather shoes. "You look marvelous, darling," she said, with a laugh as she caught her reflection in the hall mirror. She was beginning to remember a Grace without bruises, without scars, and she liked it.

When she arrived at the courthouse, Robbie was already inside. He too, was alone. Had his family deserted him, or had he wanted to face Grace one last time? She wondered. As their names were called, they entered at the same time, through the heavy wooden doors. Robbie sat to the left, Grace to the right.

Within moments, Judge Carson appeared. He nodded at the two of them, and said hello to Grace. "I must say," he began, "that I am rather disappointed in you, Mr. Gagnon. I was rather hoping to never see your face again."

As he read through the charges, he watched Robbie's facial expression. Grace watched the judge.

"So what we have here is a case of breaking and entering. That's going to cost you. A charge of attempted assault with a deadly weapon, and . . ."

"Wait a minute, Judge. I didn't have a weapon on me," Robbie hollered disrespectfully.

"Excuse me, Mr. Gagnon. Let me clarify. You have been known in the past to punch and kick Miss Preston. Your feet and your hands are your deadly weapons. Any other questions?" Judge Carson looked at Grace and smiled. He would protect her.

When he finished reading the charges, the judge asked Robbie to rise. "Mr. Gagnon, unless you have five thousand dollars handy, I'm afraid you are going to spend the next thirty days in jail, whereupon you will be transported to another location where you will receive psychological testing, and counseling. You will not be able to return here for five years. That's—let me see—1996, I believe, Mr. Gagnon. Are you pleased with yourself?"

Grace wanted to clap, as she watched Robbie sink back in his chair. Judge Carson looked at her and smiled. "Good day!" he said, as he stood up. He motioned for the court clerk to escort Robbie away.

Grace tossed her hair, turned and walked out of the courtroom. Before exiting, she turned back to Robbie. "Go to hell!" she said and walked away.

PART III - THE REBUILDING

CHAPTER 35 - OVERCOMING FEAR

During her senior year, Grace transferred from the College of Management into Psychology. She took courses in domestic violence and psychological trauma. She wrote research papers on the 'battered woman' and gave a speech in class about restraining orders and the judicial system.

However, as far as Grace had come over the past months, she continued to block out the reality of what actually happened to her.

"Grace, don't you think we should talk about what happened?" Shawn asked her one night after dinner. "I mean, you won't even let me touch you."

Grace shot him a mean look, and Shawn immediately apologized. "I didn't mean anything by that. We don't *have* to touch, but I want to get closer to you, more intimate, you know what I mean?"

"Shawn, I am over what happened. I dealt with it. Why should I go into all the gruesome details *now*? It's over with. Let it die, okay?" Grace stood and began to clear the table.

"Because, Grace, I love you. I've been reading some of your psychology books, and I know there are steps that people who were abused or traumatized go through. So far, you've gone through the first two: denial and self-blame." Shawn stood beside her, and took the dishes out of her hand.

"I said, I *dealt* with it, now leave me alone, all right?" Grace grabbed the dishes again, and walked toward her kitchen sink. "God, I hate this apartment. It reminds me so much of him," she said, as she placed the dishes in the sink.

"So let's find you another place, one where you can start fresh; one where Robbie will never enter your mind," Shawn suggested.

Over the past few months, Grace had started to become scared of her feelings for Shawn. He was getting closer to her with each passing day, and it frightened her. She was afraid to get close to anyone ever again. She was afraid to fall in love and she didn't even know what true love meant, anyway.

"Yeah, let's do that this weekend, okay? Maybe a change of scenery will do me good," Grace said, as she began to wash the dirty dishes.

Grace and Shawn sat together on the sofa for an hour after that, just holding each other. She realized that she felt safe for the first time in years. Yes, maybe she could fall in love . . . someday.

1994

Grace sat on the edge of her bed for what seemed an eternity. Her past came flooding back to her as she remembered his voice, his face—everything. She shuddered. After all this time, all these years, she was finally becoming the girl—the woman—she had always known she could be.

She had graduated from college, earning a Bachelor's degree, with a double major in psychology and sociology. She had begun speaking on domestic issues, and writing articles for the local newspaper. Just recently she was asked to be a guest speaker at her old university, in a domestic violence and trauma class.

In therapy, Grace learned that she suffered from "Post Traumatic Stress Disorder" and "Battered Woman Syndrome." She had learned a lot about herself over the past few years. She had finally overcome the low self-esteem and insecurity problems, to some extent, and had worked hard to become a major player in the financial arena.

She also worked to maintain the love of her life, Shawn. She seemed to be doing so well.

So, why was he calling her now? Reaching for the telephone, Grace replayed his message, and wrote down the phone number the operator had given her. Grace played with the idea of calling him back. But why? What could he possibly have to say? She crumpled up the piece of paper and tossed it into the trashcan. A few minutes later, she put on her lipstick and combed her hair.

As she walked out of the room and shut the door behind her, she stopped suddenly. *The final step in the healing process is closure,* she remembered her trauma professor telling her once, long ago. Here before her stood the opportunity of a lifetime. She could finally confront her abuser.

Grace turned the light back on in her room and picked up the telephone. She dialed his number. When she heard his familiar voice, her heart leaped to her throat. Everything came flooding back to her so quickly—all the hurt, the pain.

"Hello. This is Robert," he said.

"H—hello, Robbie." Grace's voice was soft and calm.

"Grace, oh wow! I didn't think you'd call. How've you been?" he asked.

Suddenly, Grace was angry. *Please don't tell me that he's calling just to say hello!* she thought. "Robert, I got your message, and I called you back. The *only* reason I called you back was to ask you *why*. I don't want to tell you how I've been, and I don't want to discuss the weather. I want to ask you if you can possibly conceive of what you've done to me?" Grace's voice remained calm.

"Grace, I called to apologize. I'm living in Colorado now. I've been through counseling and I thought enough time had passed where I could try to contact you and tell you that I'm sorry. I didn't know what I was saying before, when I apologized, but I do now. I know what I've done to you. I know how I hurt you, and I'm sorry. I really need your forgiveness, Grace. I can't live with myself anymore."

Grace was caught off-guard. She wanted to yell at him, to tell him what a living hell she had gone through for the first two years after they last saw each other. She wanted to tell him about all the nights when she woke up from a sound sleep, crying and sweating, thinking her face was bruised, or that he had once again raped her. Grace wanted him to know how she couldn't let any man close to her, physically or emotionally. And then she thought of Shawn. He was her savior and he supported her every step of the way. He was patient and never pushed for answers to his questions. He never demanded anything of her. He taught her what true love was and what it could be, when two people respected and cared for one another.

"Robert, I am older now, and much wiser. I have a new life. You are a part of my past—a part that I have worked through without your help. Therefore, I don't need—nor do I accept—your apology. I know that every counselor will tell you that to heal is to forgive. Well, I have healed. But I will not have you think that I have forgiven you. Nothing you might say could ever justify what you've done. No Robbie, apologize all you want, because it's what your counselor said would help you—but me forgive you? Never! You will have to pay for what you've done. Good-bye."

She heard Robbie's voice crack as he whispered good-bye. She laughed. When Grace hung up the phone, a wave of emotions passed through her. She had done it. She had rid herself once and for all from a tyrant—a madman. She had stood up to him for one last time, and the heavy weight that she had been carrying for so long just seemed to disappear. She was finally free.

EPILOGUE

"Grace . . . sorry I'm late, Honey! I hope you're not late for your party . . ." Mrs. Preston walked toward the hall and into Grace's bedroom, where she saw her daughter standing before the mirror, touching her cheek. "Honey, are you all right?" she asked.

"Oh. Hi, Mom. I didn't hear you come in. Yes, I'm fine—just fine. I was just reminded of another time, that's all." Grace walked away from the mirror and gave her mother a quick hug.

"Now . . . where's my granddaughter?" Mrs. Preston said, as she snuck into the adjoining bedroom.

"Shhh. Elizabeth's sleeping. She fell asleep on the way home from Mary's house. We just got in a little while ago. I got stuck at the office, so I was late picking her up. Now, I'm late for dinner. Shawn's waiting, and I haven't even finished dressing." Grace slipped on her shoes and stood in the doorway to her daughter's bedroom.

"She's my little miracle, Mom," she said, as her eyes filled with tears. "Robbie may have taken three years of my life away, but at least I'm alive. And I've got a beautiful daughter."

"Yes Honey," her mother said, "you certainly do."

Resources

By the time it takes to boil water, ten women in this country will have been physically assaulted. The reality is, a woman is beaten every 15 seconds in the United States. In Massachusetts alone, a woman is murdered by an intimate partner every nine days (*Federal Bureau of Investigation, National Census Bureau, Oct. 1992).*

Domestic violence is not going away, but you can guard yourself against getting involved with a potential abuser. Following are signs to look for in a battering personality: (provided by DOVE, a shelter for battered women, located in Quincy, Massachusetts)

1. Jealousy: At the beginning of a relationship, an abuser will always say that his jealousy is a sign of his love; jealousy has nothing to do with love. It is a sign of insecurity and possessiveness. The batterer will question the victim about who they talk to, accusations of flirting or time spent with family. As the jealousy progresses, calls may be made frequently during the day or the abuser may drop by unexpectedly. The victim may not be allowed to work for fear that the partner may meet someone else, or the abuser may even do strange things such as checking the car mileage or asking friends to watch over their partner.

2. Controlling behaviors: The batterer will say that his behavior is because of concern for your safety, the need to use time well, or the need to make good decisions. The abuser will be angry if the partner is *late* returning from the store or an appointment, and will question closely about

where the victim went and with whom they talked. As this behavior gets worse, the victim may not be allowed to make personal decisions about the house, clothing, going to church, etc.

3. Quick involvement: Many battered partners dated or knew their abuser for less than six months before they were engaged or living together.

4. Unrealistic expectations: Abusers are very dependent on their partner for all their needs—the expectation for the partner to be the perfect wife, mother, lover or friend. They will say things like, "If you loved me...I'm all you need, you're all I need." The partner is supposed to take care of everything emotionally and in the home.

5. Isolation: The abuser tries to cut the victim off from all resources. If you have friends, you are labeled with names such as whore or slut. If you are close to family, you are "tied to apron strings." The abuser accuses people who are supportive of causing trouble or may want to live in the country without a phone. Use of a car may be limited, or the abuser may try to keep the victim from working or going to school.

6. Blames others for feelings: The abuser will tell the partner, "You make me mad," or "You're hurting me by not doing what I ask..." The abuser tries to manipulate the partner.

7. Verbal abuse: In addition to saying things that are meant to be cruel or hurtful, this can be seen by the abuser as degrading the partner, cursing them, running down any of their accomplishments. The abuser will tell them they're stupid and unable to function without their presence. This may involve waking to verbal abuse or not being allowed to sleep.

8. Threats of violence: This would include any threat of physical force meant to control the partner.

9. Breaking or striking objects: This behavior is used as punishment (breaking loved possessions), but is mostly used to terrorize the partner into submission. The abuser may beat on tables with their fists, throw objects around or near the partner. Again, this is a remarkable behavior; only immature people beat on objects in the presence of others in order to threaten them.

10. Any force used during an argument: This may involve an abuser holding a partner down, physically restraining them from leaving the room, locking them in a closet, any pushing or shoving.

Types of Abuse

Abuse comes in many forms: physical, sexual, verbal, psychological and economic, to name a few. Below is a list that depicts the many kinds of abusive behavior. These are the "red flags" that should go off in your mind, if you are currently involved or know someone who portrays any of these behaviors.

1. Physical abuse - any forceful behavior such as slapping, punching, kicking, pinching, pushing, shoving, biting, use of a weapon, throwing bodily, wrestling, pulling hair, spitting, throwing objects, arm twisting, and denial of physical needs such as sleep, food or medical attention.

2. Sexual abuse - any non-consenting sexual act or behavior such as forcing oneself when she says "no", when she is sleeping, if she is drunk, manipulating, coercing, forcing by use of weapons—any touch that is unwanted, degrading or sexually attacking, exposing oneself, penetration via vaginal, oral or anal, jokes aimed to insult her.

3. Verbal abuse - any threats to do bodily harm to the victim, children, pets, or self. Threatening to punch, hit, kick, use weapons; vague threats such as, "I'm really going to let you have it...you'll be sorry." Any yelling, screaming or threats to disclose confidential information about her.

4. Psychological abuse - involves not only hurt and anger, but also fear and degradation. The object of such abuse is to render the partner emotionally helpless and insecure about her own self worth or ability to escape further abuse. Below is a brief list of psychological abuse:

- continued attacks on self-esteem
- repeated harassing, interrogating or degradation
- threats other than physical
- insults to her person
- controlling or limiting her behavior (keeping her from phone, friends)
- forcing her to stay awake
- driving her around in the car for hours
- blaming her for everything that goes wrong
- forcing her to do degrading acts such as kneeling or performing unwanted sexual acts

5. Economic abuse - refusing her access to money for food, clothing, basic needs; controlling assets such as car, credit cards, house; putting all the bills in her name and running up charges, and/or putting all the bills in her name and giving her no access to money.

MYTHS AND FACTS REGARDING DOMESTIC VIOLENCE

The following information is provided by www.famvi.com

MYTH 1: Domestic violence does not affect many people.

FACT: A woman is beaten every 15 seconds. (Bureau of Justice Statistics, Report to the nation on Crime and Justice. The Data. Washington DC Office of Justice Program, US Dept. of Justice. Oct 1983)

Domestic violence is the leading cause of injury to women between ages 15 and 44 in the United States—more than car accidents, muggings, and rapes combined. (Uniform Crime Reports, Federal Bureau of Investigation, 1991)

Battered women are more likely to suffer miscarriages and to give birth to babies with low birth weights. (Surgeon General, United States, 1992)

MYTH 2: Battering is only a momentary loss of temper.

FACT: Battering is the establishment of control and fear in a relationship through violence and other forms of abuse. The batterer uses acts of violence and a series of behaviors, including intimidation, threats, psychological abuse, isolation, etc. to coerce and control the other person. The violence may not happen often, but it remains as a hidden (and constant) terrorizing factor. (Uniform Crime Reports, Federal Bureau of Investigation, 1990)

One in five women victimized by their spouses or ex-spouses report they had been victimized over and over again by the same person. (The Basics of Batterer Treatment, Common Purpose, Inc., Jamaica Plain, MA)

MYTH 3: Domestic violence only occurs in poor, urban areas.

FACT: Women of all cultures, races, occupations, income levels, and ages are battered—by husbands, boyfriends, lovers and partners. (Surgeon General Antonia Novello, as quoted in Domestic Violence: Battered Women, publication of the Reference Department of the Cambridge Public Library, Cambridge, MA)

Approximately one-third of the men counseled (for battering) at Emerge are professional men who are well respected in their jobs and their communities. These have included doctors, psychologists, lawyers, ministers, and business executives. (For Shelter and Beyond, Massachusetts Coalition of Battered Women Service Groups, Boston, MA 1990)

MYTH 4: Domestic violence is just a push, slap or punch—it does not produce serious injuries.

FACT: Battered women are often severely injured—22 to 35 percent of women who visit medical emergency rooms are there for injuries related to ongoing partner abuse. (David Adams, "Identifying the Assaultive Husband in Court: You be the Judge." Boston Bar Journal, 33-4, July/August 1989)

One in four pregnant women have a history of partner violence. (Journal of the American Medical Association, 1992)

MYTH 5: It is easy for battered women to leave their abuser.

FACT: Women who leave their batterers are at a 75% greater risk of being killed by the batterer than those who stay. (Barbara Hart, National Coalition Against Domestic Violence, 1988)

Nationally, 50 percent of all homeless women and children are on the streets because of violence in the home. (Senator Joseph Biden, U.S. Senate Committee on the Judiciary, Violence Against Women: Victims of the System, 1991)

There are nearly three times as many animal shelters in the United States as there are shelters for battered women and their children. (Senate Judiciary Hearings, Violence Against Women Act, 1990).

Taken from "Domestic Violence: The Facts" - A Handbook to STOP Violence, Battered Women Fighting Back, Boston, MA.

National Organizations

Center for the Prevention of Sexual and Domestic Violence
1914 North 34th Street, Suite 105
Seattle, WA 98103
(206) 634-1903

Family Violence and Sexual Assault Institute
1310 Clinic Drive
Tyler, Texas 75701
(903) 543-5100

Family Violence Prevention Fund
383 Rhode Island Street, Suite 304
San Francisco, CA 94103
(415) 252-8900

National Clearinghouse on Child Abuse and Neglect
PO Box 1182
Washington, DC 20013
(800) 394-3366

National Clearinghouse on Family Violence
Social Services Branch, Health and Welfare Canada
Ottawa, Ontario
(613) 957-2938

National Coalition Against Domestic Violence
PO Box 18749
Denver, Colorado 80218
(303) 839-1852

National Criminal Justice Resource Service
(800) 851-3420

National Training Project, Duluth Domestic Abuse
206 West Fourth Street
Duluth, MN 55806
(218) 722-2781

Battered Women's Justice Project
4032 Chicago Avenue, South
Minneapolis, MN
(800) 903-0111

INTERNATIONAL ORGANIZATIONS

Human Rights Watch
1522 K Street NW #910
Washington, DC 20005
(202) 371-6592

International Women's Rights Action Watch
Humphrey Institute of Public Affairs
University of Minnesota
301 19th Avenue, South
Minneapolis, MN 55455

United National Development Fund for Women
(UNEFEM)
304 E. 45th Street
New York, NY 10017
(212) 906-6400

STATE COALITIONS LIST

If you, or someone you know, are being abused, you are not alone. There are services that can help you. They are provided below.

National Coalition Against Domestic Violence
P.O. Box 18749
Denver, CO 80218
Phone: 303-839-1852
Fax: 303-831-9251

National Coalition Against Domestic Violence
Public Policy Office
1532 16th Street, NW
Washington, D.C. 20036
Phone: 202-745-1211
Fax: 202-745-0088

National Network to End Domestic Violence, Inc.
660 Pennsylvania Avenue, SE
Suite 303
Washington, DC 20003
Phone: 202-543-5566
Fax: 202-543-5626

Alabama Coalition Against Domestic Violence
P.O. Box 4762
Montgomery, AL 36101
Phone: 334-832-4842
Fax: 334-832-4803

Alaska Network on Domestic Violence
and Sexual Assault
130 Seward, Room 209
Juneau, Alaska 99801
Phone: (907) 586-3650

Arizona Coalition Against Domestic Violence
100 West Camelback Street, Suite 109
Phoenix, AZ 85013
Phone: 602-279-2900
Fax: 602-279-2980

Arkansas Coalition Against Domestic Violence
#1 Sheriff Lane, Suite C
North Little Rock, AR 72114
Phone: 501-812-0571
Fax: 501-812-0578

California Alliance Against Domestic Violence
926 J Street, Suite 1000
Sacramento CA 95814
Telephone 916-444-7163 or 800-524-4765
Fax 916-444-7165
e-mail caadv@cwo.com
http://www.caadv.org

California Alliance Against Domestic Violence
- Southern Office
8929 S. Sepulveda Blvd., Suite 520
Los Angeles CA 90045-3605
Phone 310-649-2479
Fax 310-649-3953

Statewide California Coalition for Battered Women
3711 Long Beach Blvd., #718
Long Beach, CA 90807
Phone: 562/981-1202
Fax: 981-3202
Toll-free: 888/722-2952
e-mail: sccbw@sccbw.org

Colorado Coalition Against Domestic Violence
P.O. Box 18902
Denver, CO 80218
Phone: 303-831-9632
Fax: 303-832-7067

Connecticut Coalition Against Domestic Violence
106 Pitken Street
East Hartford, CT 06108
Phone: 860-282-7899
Fax: 860-282-7892
800-281-1481 (In State)
888-774-2900 (In State Hotline)

DC Coalition Against Domestic Violence
513 U Street, NW
Washington, DC 20001
202-387-5630 (phone)
202-387-5684 (fax)
dccadv@aol.com (email)

Delaware Coalition Against Domestic Violence
100 West 10th Street, Suite 703
Wilmington, DE 19801
Phone: 302-658-2958
Fax: 302-658-5049

Florida Coalition Against Domestic Violence
308 E. Park Avenue
Tallahassee, FL 32301
Phone: (850) 425-2749
Fax: (850) 425-3091
TDD: (850) 621-4202
In-state: 800-500-1119

Georgia Coalition on Family Violence
1827 Powers Ferry Road, Bldg 3, Suite 325
Atlanta, GA 30339
Phone: 770-984-0085
Fax: 770-984-0068
800-334-2836 (In State Hotline)

Hawaii State Coalition Against Domestic Violence
98-939 Moanalua Road
Aiea, HI 96701-5012
Phone: 808-486-5072
Fax: 808-486-5169

Idaho Coalition Against Sexual and Domestic Violence
815 Park Blvd., Suite 140
Boise, ID 83712
Phone: 208-384-0419
Fax: 208-331-0687
E-mail: domvio@micron.net

Illinois Coalition Against Domestic Violence
801 S. 11th St.
Springfield, IL 62703
Phone: 217-789-2830
Fax: 217-789-1939

Indiana Coalition Against Domestic Violence
2511 E. 46th Street, Suite N-3
Indianapolis, IN 46205
TOLL-FREE: 800-332-7385
Phone: 317-543-3908
Fax: 317-377-7050

Iowa Coalition Against Domestic Violence
2603 Bell Avenue, Suite 100
Des Moines, IA 50321
Phone: 515-244-8028
Fax: 515-244-7417
In-State Hotline (Not part of Coalition) 800-942-0333

Kansas Coalition Against Sexual and Domestic Violence
220 SW 33rd Street, Suite 100
Topeka, KS 66611
Phone: 785-232-9784
Fax: 785-266-1874

Kentucky Domestic Violence Association
P.O. Box 356
Frankfort, KY 40602
Phone: 502-695-2444
Fax: 502-695-2488

Louisiana Coalition Against Domestic Violence
P.O. Box 77308
Baton Rouge, LA 70879
Phone: 225-752-1296
Fax: 222-751-8927

Maine Coalition to End Domestic Violence
128 Main Street
Bangor, ME 04401
Phone: 207-941-1194
Fax: 207-941-2327

Maryland Network Against Domestic Violence
6911 Laurel Bowie Road, Suite 309
Bowie, MD 20715
TOLL-FREE: 800-MD-HELPS
Phone: 301-352-4574
Fax: 301-809-0422

Massachusetts Coalition Against Sexual Assault and Domestic Violence
Jane Doe, Inc.
14 Beacon Street, Suite 507
Boston, MA 02108
Phone: 617-248-0922
Fax: 617-248-0902

Michigan Coalition Against Domestic & Sexual Violence
3893 Okemos Road, Ste B2
Okemos MI 48864
Phone: 517-347-7000
Fax: 517-347-1377

Minnesota Coalition for Battered Women
450 North Syndicate Street, Suite 122
St. Paul, MN 55104
Phone: 612-646-6177
Fax: 612-646-1527
Toll-free: (800) 289-6177

Mississippi State Coalition Against Domestic Violence
P.O. Box 4703
Jackson, MS 39296-4703
Toll-Free: 800-898-3234
Phone: 601-981-9196
Fax: 601-981-2501

Missouri Coalition Against Domestic Violence
415 East McCarty
Jefferson City, MO 65101
Phone: 573-634-4161
Fax: 573-636-3728

Montana Coalition Against Domestic
and Sexual Violence
Child Advocacy Project
P.O. Box 633
Helena, MT 59624
Phone: 406.443.7794
Fax: 406.443.7818
mcadsv@mt.net

Nebraska Domestic Violence
and Sexual Assault Coalition
825 M Street, Suite 404
Lincoln, NE 68508-2253
In-State Toll Free: 800-876-6238
Phone: 402-476-6256
Fax: 402-476-6806

Nevada Network Against Domestic Violence
100 West Grove Street, Suite 315
Reno, NV 89509
TOLL-FREE: 800-230-1955
Phone: 775-828-1115
Fax: 775-828-9911

New Hampshire Coalition Against Domestic
and Sexual Violence
P.O. Box 353
Concord, NH 03302-0353
In-State Toll Free: 800-852-3388
Phone: 603-224-8893
Fax: 603-228-6096

New Jersey Coalition for Battered Women
2620 Whitehorse Hamilton Square Road
Trenton, NJ 08690
TOLL-FREE: for Battered Lesbians: 800-224-0211
(in NJ only)
In-State Toll Free: 800-572-7233
Phone: 609-584-8107
Fax: 609-584-9750

New Mexico State Coalition Against Domestic Violence
114 Oak NE
Albuquerque, NM 87106
Toll-Free: 800-773-3645 (in NM Only)
Phone: 505-246-9240
Fax: 505-246-9434

New York State Coalition Against Domestic Violence
79 Central Avenue
Albany, NY 12206
Toll-free: 800-942-6906
Toll-free (Spanish): 800-942-6908
Phone: 518-432-4864
Fax: 518-463-3155
E-mail: nyscadv@aol.com

North Carolina Coalition Against Domestic Violence
115 Market Street, Suite 400
Durham, NC 27707
Phone: 919-956-9124
Fax: 919-682-1449

North Dakota Council on Abused Women's Services
State Networking Office
418 East Rosser Avenue, Suite 320
Bismarck, ND 58501-4046
Toll-free: 800-472-2911 (In ND Only)
Phone: 701-255-6240
Fax: 701-255-1904

Ohio Domestic Violence Network
4041 North High Street, Suite 400
Columbus, OH 43214-3247
Toll-free: 800-934-9840
Phone: 614-784-0023
Fax: 614-784-0033
E-mail: todvn@ee.net

Oklahoma Coalition Against Domestic Violence
and Sexual Assault
2525 NW Expressway, Suite 101
Oklahoma City, OK 73112
Phone: 405-848-1815
Fax: 405-848-3469
Toll-free: 1-800-522-7233

Oregon Coalition Against Domestic and Sexual Violence
659 Cottage St NE
Salem, OR 97301
Phone: 503-365-9644
Fax: 503-566-7870
E-mail: ocadsv@teleport.com

Pennsylvania Coalition Against Domestic Violence/
National Resource Center on Domestic Violence
Resource Center on Domestic Violence
6400 Flank Drive, Suite 1300
Harrisburg, PA 17112-2778
Toll-free: 800-932-4632
Phone: 717-545-6400
Fax: 717-671-8149

(Puerto Rico)
Coordinadora Paz para la Mujer, Inc
Proyecto Coalicion Contra la Violencia Domestica
P.O. Box 1007 RMS 108
San Juan, Puerto Rico 00919
Telefone: (787) 281-7579
Tel./Fax: (787) 767-6843
Correo electronico: pazparalamujer@yunque.net

Rhode Island Coalition Against Domestic Violence
422 Post Road, Suite 202
Warwick, RI 02888
Toll-free: 800-494-8100 (in state only)
Phone: 401-467-9940
Fax: 401-467-9943

South Carolina Coalition Against Domestic Violence
and Sexual Assault
P.O. Box 7776
Columbia, SC 29202-7776
Toll-free: 800-260-9293
Phone: 803-750-1222
Fax: 803-750-1246

South Dakota Coalition Against Domestic Violence
and Sexual Assault
P.O. Box 141
Pierre, SD 57501
Toll-free: 800-572-9196
Phone: 605-945-0869
Fax: 605-945-0870

Tennessee Coalition Against Domestic
and Sexual Violence
P.O. Box 120972
Nashville, TN 37212
Office: 615) 386-9406
Fax: (615) 383-2967
Toll-free Information Line: (800) 289-9018 (8 a.m. - 5 p.m. M-F)
Statewide Domestic Violence and Child Abuse Hotline: (800) 356-6767
Email: tcadsv@telelink.net

Texas Council on Family Violence
8701 P.O. Box 16180
Austin, TX 78716
Phone: 512-794-1133
Fax: 512-794-1199

Utah Domestic Violence Advisory Council
120 North 200 West, #319
Salt Lake City, UT 84103
Toll-free: 800-897-LINK (in state only)
Phone: 801-538-4635
Fax: 801-538-4016

Vermont Network Against Domestic Violence
and Sexual Assault
P.O. Box 405
Montpelier, VT 05601
Phone: 802-223-1302
Fax: 802-223-6943

Virginians Against Domestic Violence
2850 Sandy Bay Road, Suite 101
Williamsburg, VA 23185
Toll-free: 800-838-VADV
Phone: 757-221-0990
Fax: 757-229-1553

Washington State Coalition Against Domestic Violence
8645 Martin Way NE
Suite 103
Lacey, WA 98516
Phone: 360/407-0756
Fax: 360/407-0761
TTY: 360/407-0760

West Virgina Coalition Against Domestic Violence
Elk Office Center
4710 Chimney Drive, Suite A
Charleston, WV 25302
Phone: 304-965-3552
Fax: 304-965-3572
Website: www.wvcadv.org

Wisconsin Coalition Against Domestic Violence
307 South Paterson, Suite 1
Madison, WI 53703
Phone: 608-255-0539
Fax: 608-255-3560

Wyoming Coalition Against Domestic Violence
and Sexual Assault
P.O. Box 236
Laramie, WY 82073
Phone: 307-755-5481
Fax: 307-755-5482

National Domestic Violence/Abuse
HOTLINE: 800-799-7233

Support Network for Battered Women
HOTLINE - 800-572-2782

Friends of Battered Women
and Their Children
HOTLINE - 800-603-HELP

Good Samaritan Homeless Center
for Women and Children
HOTLINE - 800-448-0636